Ancient Scrolls

MICHAEL AVI-YONAH

PALPHOT

Copyright © 1994 by G.G. The Jerusalem Publishing House, Ltd.
39, Tchernechovski St. Jerusalem, Israel.

Distribution by Palphot Marketing Ltd.
10, Hahagana St. Herzlia, Israel.
Tel: 972-9-555238; Fax: 972-9-571701

ISBN 965-280-119-4

Printed in Israel

CONTENTS

ILLUSTRATION SOURCES

Israel Department of Antiquities and Museums p. 5, 6, 7, 10, 11, 19, 20, 39, 56, 57, 61; The British Museum p. 7, 8, 12, 13, 22, 23, 47, 51; Oriental Institute, University of Chicago p. 15; Hirmer Fotoarchiv, Munich p. 50; Biblioteca Medicea Laurenziana, Firenze, Dr. Pineider p. 36; Bayerische Staatsbibliothek, Munich p. 42; Bibliothèque Nationale, Paris p. 40, 44; Biblioteca Nazionale, Venezia p. 45; The Dumbarton Oaks Collection p. 46; Yad Ben-Zvi, Jerusalem p. 50; The Shrine of the Book, Israel Museum p. 60, 61, 65, 66, 67, 69, 71, 73; Biblioteca Ambrosiana, Milano p. 41, 42; Floersheim Trust p. 53; The Jewish National Library, Jerusalem p. 25, 52; Cairo Museum p. 14; The Israel Museum, Jerusalem p. 30; R. Nowitz p. 28, 29.

The Means For Ancient Communication

The discovery of writing, and in particular of alphabetic writing, marked a turning-point in the development of civilization. In fact it marked the dividing line between pre-history and history proper. It enabled mankind to develop a new manner of communication, amplifying the traditional word-of-mouth method. Communication was now possible across both space (because writing could be sent from one place to another) and time (because writing could be preserved for later generations). The first evidence of the new art of writing has come to us from temple records in Mesopotamia, in which the property of the sanctuary was carefully recorded, and from Egypt on the sealings of jars and other objects as a way of marking royal ownership.

1. Stone

As writing developed, the materials for it were differentiated. Some were meant to ensure permanence, others were temporary expedients adopted in order to save the more expensive writing materials for the permanent records. The materials used for writing can be divided (as in the panel game) into animal, vegetable and mineral. Stone was used mainly for monumental inscriptions but occasionally also for notebooks; for instance the Athenian schoolboys used slate tablets as exercise books, scratching with a sharp point the letters they learned. But in general we may say that writing on stone was mainly intended for public display, for the monumental and the permanent. As writing on stone is done with hammer and chisel, the best way to cut in the signs on the stone surface is to strike it with the chisel held in the left hand, and the hammer in the right.

Epitaph of Uzziah, King of Judah (late Second Temple period)—stone inscription: "hence we brought the bones of Uzziah, King of Judah, and not to be opened."

5

Hence the stroke goes from right to left and the writing develops in that direction. The Semitic languages, Hebrew and Arabic among them, still stick to this old way of writing from right to left.

2. Metal

On the whole, metal sheets were rarely used for writing. Because of the expense of the material, the metal was often melted down in less prosperous times and thus, few of the sheets remained. Sometimes metal was employed to give permanence to a record, apart from occasional royal extravagances such as writing on sheets of gold or silver, especially in foundation tablets. Examples of writing on gold were found in the Second Temple in Jerusalem. But there are two metals which were more commonly used. Bronze or copper

Left: Inscription carved on a stone found in Caesarea mentioning the name of Pontius Pilate
Below: Two copper scrolls as they were found in cave 3, in Qumran.

Strip cut from a copper scroll. As a result of oxidisation of the copper, the scroll could not be unrolled, so it was cut into long strips.

was supposed to give permanence to the record, and when used in tablets these could be more or less conveniently stored. In fact the archives of most of the Greek states and the old Roman archives consisted of row upon row of bronze tablets on which the treaties and the decrees were carefully inscribed. Soldiers dismissed honourably from the Roman army after long service had their citizenship rights recorded on small bronze tablets, the so-called diplomas, of which many have been found, giving valuable information on the names of the units and their posting. The copper scrolls found in one of the Qumran caves were intended, because of the use of this special material and by the marks indicating that the "scrolls" once had the form of a tablet which was fixed to a wall, to form a permanent record. On the other hand their contents are a quite fantastic list of treasures, and the queer fact that this list of untold riches was apparently meant to be displayed on a wall casts some doubts upon the reality of this treasure; but then the use of bronze makes no sense. The whole matter is a puzzle.

Apart from bronze, lead was used for writing and sometimes also silver. Lead, a heavy, dull metal which—although the ancients did not know it — was poisonous, was used for a special purpose: for cursing. Execration tablets, supposed to have a magic influence, were written on lead.

3. Wood

Archives of bronze tablets need lots of space, and it was in general difficult to file inscriptions on stone or metal. It was somewhat easier to do so with wood. We have no record in antiquity of anything resembling the collections of texts on tablets of light palm wood of

Roman military diploma engraved on a bronze tablet

7

Wooden board with advertisements, written in Greek

which some of the Buddhist libraries in the East are composed; wooden boards were, however, used for public display. Whitened boards (the so-called album) were used for public notices in the Greek and Roman periods. If the notice became out of date, the board could be whitewashed again, and a new inscription written on it. It should be remembered for instance that it was a wooden tablet on which the inscription "Jesus of Nazareth King of the Jews" was written in Latin, Greek and Hebrew (or Aramaic) above the cross of Jesus at the Crucifixion. Slaves were also sold

below similar tablets advertising their qualities. But of course such use of wood was strictly temporary and not many such tablets have been preserved. In the climate prevailing in most countries of the ancient world, apart from Egypt, wood was not a permanent material.

4. Wax Tablets

Another way of making temporary records was by scratching on wax tablets. Wooden frames, covered with wax, were held together by a ring so they could be turned like the pages of a book. The Latin word for such a group of tablets, codex, has become the common appellation of a book composed of sheets, as we shall see further on. Wax tablets were used as notebooks, or for any kind of writing of a temporary nature. Sometimes, as at Pompeii, even contracts for loans or other banking records were written on wax. The tablets were then carefully sealed, the witnesses signing near the seals. After a record of the contents had been made on the outside of the tablets they were held by the banker as evidence of a loan. But of course such records, although in theory permanent, were in practice needed

Right: *A statue of an Egyptian scribe*
Left: *Wax tablets joined together to form a codex*

An Aramaic or early Parthian ostracon from Nisa (Turkmenistan)

Ostracon with Hebrew alphabet. Scroll fragment from Leviticus (26:2-16)

only until the debt was settled. The wax tablets were written upon with a sharp tool, the so-called stylus (hence our word for the "style" of an author). It had one sharp end for writing and one broad one for smoothing out the surface of the wax and erasing the writing, so that a tablet could be used again and again. Wax tablets were the common notebooks of antiquity. We are told that the Emperor Caligula had tablets in several colours, including red and black; on these his secretaries noted down the names of those who were to be executed by the sword or poisoned — all according to the colour of the tablets. But of course he and other less bloodthirsty rulers must also have had normal wax tablets to make notes for daily use. The tablets were often bound together by twos or threes; they were called diptychs if of two leaves, triptychs if of three.

5. Ostraca

Another kind of writing on what was meant to be provisional material has proved surprisingly permanent, the so-called ostraca. Among the most common objects in antiquity, as they still are, are the broken sherds of a pot. Useless in themselves, they were made of fired clay, practically indestructible. Hence, they were

Stylus used for writing on wax tablets

Inscribed ostracon from Lachish, about 586 BC

commonly used for writing letters, or short messages or lists or receipts, anything of a more or less temporary nature used and then thrown away. However, very often it was their fate to be unearthed in excavations, thus surviving the centuries. The contents of the Hebrew ostraca of biblical times, like those found at Lachish, at Arad and at Jerusalem, are of the greatest importance, both for our knowledge of the Hebrew script and as regards the light they throw on the political and, in particular, the economic life of the period. The same is true of ostraca all over the ancient world. There are tens of thousands of them known, especially in Egypt, where they were commonly used for tax receipts. As taxes had to be paid every year, the receipts did not need to be kept for a very long time. They would be put in some convenient place and then thrown away on the next rubbish heap, to be unearthed by the spade of the excavators in later ages. For example, an interesting ostracon from Shivta in the Negev recorded that X had done his civic duty by labouring one day to clean the public water reservoirs.

6. Clay Tablets

Now we come to the more permanent forms of writing. One of those known from Babylonia, but not continued beyond ancient times, was clay tablets, which cease about the beginning of the Christian era. They were probably an invention of the Sumerians in southern Babylonia, where there was plenty of the raw material. Tablets fashioned of clay were first used for noting down temple property; then they became a general means of written communication throughout Mesopotamia and the whole ancient East. Even the pharaohs corresponded with their Canaanite vassals on clay - witness the el-Amarna archives of the 15th-14th centuries BC. The tablets were usually fashioned in two parts: the tablet proper, which was the inner core, and a clay envelope on which the text of the inner tablet was recorded again. Normally only the outside needed to be consulted; but in case of emergency the envelope could be broken and the original record read. The writing was done with a sharp instrument of wood or metal in the form known to us as cuneiform (from the Latin cunus, wedge), because of the wedge-shaped character of the signs which composed the various marks. Originally cuneiform writing was a pictorial one, but for technical reasons the signs gradually developed into a sort of abbreviated memory sign of the original picture, which was broken down and arranged by wedge-shaped strokes; Chinese writing has devel-

A cuneiform tablet

A relief of Hammurabi with cuneiform texts

oped on parallel lines. Because of the particular nature of this material, and the type of writing, it does not matter in cuneiform whether you write from right to left, left to right, top to bottom; any direction is good enough provided the sequence of sign is observed. The completed tablets were placed in an oven and baked; the result was a very hard piece of clay which has endured. Clay tablets have been found by the thousands in excavations, in Mesopotamia, and a few also in other countries — at Gezer and Taanach in Israel, for instance. There are about a million tablets known in the various museums, and of course there must have been very many more.

7. Papyrus

The fourth type of writing material which belongs to the "vegetable" realm — like the wooden tablets — was papyrus. This was apparently invented in Egypt, where the papyrus reed grows along the banks of the Nile, especially in the delta. The papyrus plant was in fact used as the symbol of the country of Lower Egypt in general. The plant, however, not only served as a source of writing material but supplied an astonishing number of the other needs of the inhabitants of ancient Egypt. Fuel, food, medicine, clothes, rugs, sails, ropes, even a kind of chewing gum were made from the reed or its leaves. In this particular case—to wit, its use for writing— the method of employing papyrus was to cut the outer ring away from the lower stem. Then the inside core of the papyrus reed was peeled off, strip after strip. The single strips were laid side by side, and then another layer laid over them at right angles. The two layers were beaten with a broad-headed mallet so that the single leaves were fused into sheets, which formed a very strong and flat writing surface. Further papyrus strips could be arranged on each sheet — one row horizontal, and then another vertical row at the back of the sheet. As a result the papyrus gained a certain cohesion. Moreover, as the horizontal strips, the ones used mainly for writing, were so arranged that each overlapped the one above it, the scribe's pen travelled down over the surface of the papyrus, which made writing much easier. Once dried, the sheets of papyrus were polished with pumice, and cut to standard sizes. The single sheets could be used

as letters or for notes; to produce a book, a number of sheets were used, stuck together to form a scroll. It is interesting to note that the quality of the papyrus in Egypt, far from improving as time went on, rather declined. The fine and even papyrus of the Ramesaic period is the best; after that comes the heavier and thicker Ptolemaic papyrus and then the clumsy and coarse variety of the Roman period. In general the "front", with the horizontally arranged leaves, was kept on the inside of the scroll and the "back" on the outside. As the inside of the papyrus was written before the outside, we call the inside the *recto*, or right side, and the outside the *verso*, or back part, although both could be equally well used. Usually the first writing on a papyrus was on the recto; but occasionally, for utilitarian purposes, the verso was used — for instance when the archives of some village or province were bursting with out-of-date papyrus rolls, these were sold as so much waste paper; the sheets were then divided between schools, offices and other institutions, where they were

Below: *Egyptian writing on papyrus*

A scribe's set of writing instruments, Egyptian, Ist Dynasty.

reversed and what had been the verso was re-used for writing.

The consumption of papyrus in the Egyptian offices was enormous—it is recorded that

the office of the Finance Minister Appolonius, who served Ptolemy 11 of Egypt (3rd century BC), used up 434 rolls in 33 days. This is amazing; though of course it is quite possible that a good number of the expensive rolls were stolen and passed into private hands.

For literary works or longer texts, the sheets of papyrus were stuck together. Care had to be taken that one horizontal or vertical side should follow another and the sides should not be mixed up. The sizes of papyrus sheets were standardized, just as paper sizes are today. They were graded from what Pliny calls the Augustian or imperial chart and others, and run from the royal format (*carta regia*) to the commercial size, which was much smaller. The single sheets were combined into rolls, the normal format being about twenty sheets to one roll, although we know of much longer rolls, up to 133 feet. For practical purposes this was not convenient. When one had to hold the roll in the right hand and re-roll it with the left, reading column after column of text, the inconvenience of very long rolls is very apparent. Hence we see why the normal roll, which is about 35 ft. long, was much more common. This prescribed size explains why certain books of the Old Testament, such as the Books of Samuel or Kings or Chronicles, were divided into two parts; the whole book would have been too big to be held conveniently. On the other hand the books of the twelve minor prophets were put together in a single scroll, although they differ so much in content. The same is true of the Greek Bible and of the writings of Homer, where the Iliad and Odyssey were divided into 24 books, corresponding to one roll each.

The writing on the papyrus rolls was done with a reed dipped in ink. The Greek word *calamos* for reed has become in Hebrew *culmus*; the pen-and ink holder is still called *calmar* from the same root, used mostly in excusing scribal errors — "pelitat ha-Culmus" meaning literally a "slip of the pen". The Greeks improved on the Egyptian method by taking reeds of hard material which could be conveniently slit in two. The ink was composed of lamp-black, with gum and water; it is very durable, as one can see from the extant papyri, but sometimes some metallic component was used which corroded the papyrus.

From Egypt writing on papyrus came to Phoenicia, and the Phoenicians brought it to Greece. We know that the Greeks learnt about papyrus rolls from the Phoenicians, because the Greek word for papyrus is *biblos*, from Byblos, the Greek name of the old city of Gebal in Phoenicia. Byblos meant at first the town, and then the papyrus which came by way of it, and then any book in general — in the plural several books were called *biblia* (plural of *biblos*), and so gradually we get the word *Bible* for the Holy Script, *The Book*.

The completed scrolls were stored by one of two methods. They could be kept on open shelves in libraries, each one provided with a little tag for identification, or placed rolled up in boxes. Each box normally held a "decade" of 10 standard scrolls, which explains why in the case of Pliny's History of Rome, for example, whole groups of ten books have been lost, while other groups of equal size have been preserved. In Palestine papyri were apparently employed as early as the Canaanite period, although we have no direct evidence of this. Later on, papyrus might have been used for the writing of the Prophetic books. In any case the Israelite administration, as well as that in the neighbouring country of Arabia or Nabataea, used papyrus. We have evidence from excavations that documents were written on papyrus, rolled up, tied with a string and sealed with a clay stamp on which a seal impression was made. Usually only the seal impressions have been preserved, while the much more valuable documents themselves have disappeared. The seal impressions bear a mark or design which can be deciphered, and we should be thankful for this fact.

8. Parchment

The chief rival of papyrus as a writing material was parchment made from skins. Records of writing on leather skins exist from the early Assyrian period, and occasionally such rolls have also been found in Egypt. The oldest surviving text on skin is said to be a roll from the time of the Egyptian 12th Dynasty, now in Berlin. The Persians according to Herodotus, used "royal hides" for their historical records, and the archives of one of the Persian satraps of Egypt, Arsham, of the 5th century BC, were written on leather or parch-

Painting of a man holding a scroll and standing between two Egyptian deities. Roman period, Egypt.

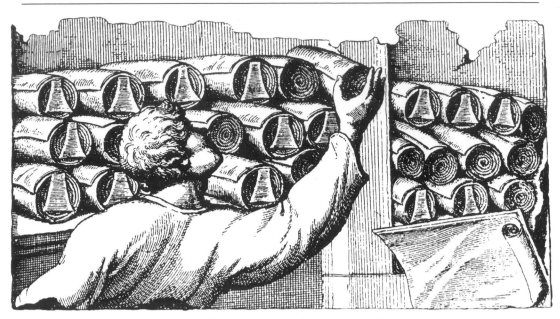

Relief showing librarian handling scrolls. Note tags attached to the scrolls.

ment. Actually parchment is technically different from leather, which is prepared by tanning. Up to a certain point animal skins for both uses are treated and worked over in the same way. Both are washed, soaked, cleansed of flesh and hair and smoothed carefully; but after that leather proper is soaked in vegetable matter containing tannin (that is to say, it is "tanned"), whereas parchment is dressed with alum and dusted with sifted chalk. The skins of sheep and goats are the normal raw material of parchment; *vellum* is the technical expression for the finer skins of calf and kid.

In ancient Judah the use of parchment is attested to about 750 BC, the date of one of the Hebrew manuscripts found in the Muraba'at cave, one of the caves near the Dead Sea. Assyrian records on parchment are in evidence from 721 BC onwards. In the biblical period parchment was used for writings of a more permanent nature, whereas normally papyrus was still used for administrative records. Anything of a greater literary or religious importance, such as the scrolls of the Law or the sayings of the Prophets, had to be written upon a more durable material. We know this from the vivid story in the book of Jeremiah, chapter XXXVI, 23 where we are told that King Jehoiakim sent Jehudi, his secretary, to fetch the roll which contained Jeremiah's words. The Bible continues: And Jehudi read in the ears of the king and it came to pass "...that when Jehudi had read three or four leaves, he (the king) cut it with the penknife, and (he) cast it into the fire that was on the hearth," and so on till the whole scroll was destroyed. Of course like most attempts to eliminate writings unpleasant to the mighty by banning them, this too miscarried and the words of Jeremiah have come down to us, Jehoiakim notwithstanding.

If the writing had been on a papyrus scroll, the king could easily have torn it up or simply flung the whole thing into the fire to be consumed by the flames, for papyrus, being vegetable material, burns easily. There would have been no need to "cut it with the penknife". It must therefore have been a roll of more durable material.

Israel was not the only country where skins were employed for this purpose. When in the 2nd century BC the Egyptian King Ptolemy II waged war upon Eumenes, King of Pergamon, a kingdom in north-western Asia Minor, we are told that he prohibited the export of papyrus to his enemy's kingdom, hoping that the absence of writing material would paralyse the machinery of government and force King Eumenes to capitulate. Ptolemy probably acted from the experience of his own administration in Egypt, which, as we have seen, consumed enormous quantities of papyrus. But as has been shown all throughout history, up until our own times, a nation with any ingenuity is able to extract advantage from such adversity, and the people of Pergamon were no excep-

Inkstand from Qumran

Table and bench found in largest room of the Essenes' building at Qumran.

tion. Forced to find a new form of writing material, they took the skins of young animals, which they scraped thin, polished and whitened. The results were excellent, even if the material was rather expensive. The skins thus prepared for writing became known as "parchment", from the Latin word *pergamentum* literally "writing material from Pergamon". This story is told by the Roman author Varro; it has been justly classed as apocryphal by modern scholars who point out that the use of skins for writing considerably antedates, as we have seen, the 2nd century BC.

Moreover the word *pergamentum* first appears in an edict of the Emperor Diocletian, who reigned in the late 3rd and in the early 4th centuries AD. The true origin of the word might be that there was a state factory for this material at Pergamon in the time of Diocletian. Whatever the case, the name parchment has stuck.

Parchment differs in various ways from papyrus as writing material. It is much more durable and can stand harder usage; papyrus rolls were easily torn and had to be frequently recopied. Parchment stands wear and tear and the ravages of time better on the whole. The parchment rolls naturally have a "flesh" side and a "hair" side. These are true recto and verso sides, unlike the artificial ones of the papyrus sheets, where the only difference is whether the leaves have been laid horizontally or vertically, which has no practical effect on the facility of writing. In parchment, the hair side—that is to say, the outside of the skin where the hair once grew—differs in colour and in fineness from the flesh side or inside, which was naturally the smoother, because no hair had to be removed from it. Hence this was originally employed for the writing, while the hair side was left for the outside of the book or scroll.

II Scrolls and Books

This brings us to the reason for the use of papyrus or of parchment in different shapes, rolls as opposed to books. As we have seen, papyrus was used mainly in scrolls, with the leaves stuck together to form a long strip of writing surface, subdivided only by the columns of equal length and width made by the scribe. Incidentally, it should be mentioned that the first leaf of a papyrus roll was called in Greek *protocollon*, from the word collon, "glue". The protocollon was the first leaf, glued on one side to the rest of the scroll but free on the other. The title of the book was sometimes written on it; this has given rise to our word protocol, the rules and customs in official life which introduce, so to speak, the substance of the negotiations. In the begin-

ning parchment also was used in scrolls. In Qumran, for instance, the documents were written on leather parchment, the single sheets being sewn together as if they had been papyrus sheets. Until this day the sacred Torah scrolls of the Jewish Law (the Five Books of Moses) used in synagogues are made up of sheets of fine parchment sewn together to form rolls. This usage has been consecrated by Jewish tradition. The scroll of the Torah, carefully written by hand, is regarded as something very sacred—scrolls have to be saved from a burning building as if they were human beings; they are transferred from one community to another if the former is dissolved, and spoiled scrolls are carefully buried.

Nevertheless the roll has certain disadvan-

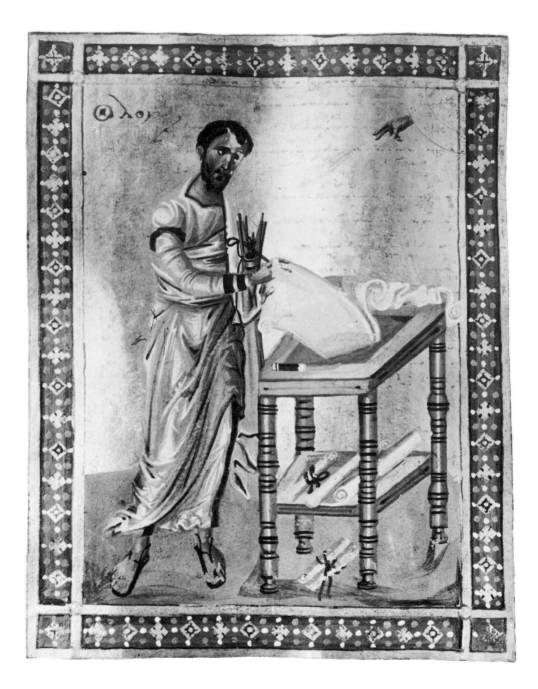

St Matthew portrayed in a Byzantine miniature as a scribe with parchment scroll.

tages, although it looks good and is easy to handle when read through from beginning to end. The reader holds it in his left hand and unrolls it with his right, then closes it by rolling it up with his left. But if the work written in the roll has to be referred to constantly, and different sections of it at different times, the rolling back and forth can become very tiring to the reader and eventually damaging to the scroll. A lawyer who needed to refer to different paragraphs in various parts of a law book, or a preacher seeking one reference after another in the Bible, would have to spend most of his time rolling the scrolls backwards and forwards, and inevitably damaging them in the process. Even when papyrus was still in general use the habit grew of abandoning the old method of attaching one sheet to another, and instead folding the individual sheets in the middle (usually taking 8 sheets divided into 16 pages) and placing the single sheets one within the other. This arrangement is called "quire", from the Latin word *quaternio*. The folded leaves were stitched at the back to hold them together. For a complete work the single quires were put side by side in their proper order, stitched at the back and bound together almost in the way with which we were familiar before the coming of the modern paperback, which has its sheets glued together and therefore soon falls apart if used regularly. Such books made from single sheets were in ancient times called a codex, from the way in which the sheets were folded together like wax tablets. As most of the early codices were lawbooks the word codex came to mean "a Book of Laws". Many ancient Bible manuscripts were also technically prepared in codex form; one of the most famous is called the Codex Sinaiticus.

A page from the Codex Sinaiticus

Moses reading from an unfolded scroll. Fresco in synagogue at Dura Europos. 244-5 AD

III Ancient Manuscripts

Texts on both papyri and parchment were written in columns, running from top to bottom, and continuing from one sheet to another. Sometimes there were two columns to a sheet, and sometimes only one. The scribe marked out carefully in advance his writing space and lines - this was particularly so in the case of parchment scrolls, where he would take a sharp penknife and, using a ruler, lightly scratch in two vertical lines for the margins, that is to say for the beginning and the end of a column. He then measured within these two vertical lines the number of horizontal lines which he could allow for each column, leaving wide margins at top and bottom, and then marked these too with a faint line, on which he proceeded to write. In the Qumran Scrolls, for instance, these marks can be clearly seen. They pass across the tops of the Hebrew letters, the letters being, as it were, suspended from this line; this is the normal method used in Hebrew scrolls. In other languages the writing was on top of the line, there being comparatively few deep descending letters.

"Shelah Lekha" (Numbers 13-15) with vowels, accents and masora, written on parchment in 1106. The oldest Hebrew biblical manuscript in the Jewish National and University Library.

Until the invention of printing, every book in existence was an original "manuscript", from the Latin *manu scriptum*, something written by hand.

1. Copying Manuscripts

There were two ways of making manuscript books. A scholar in the days before printing, if he wanted a book for himself, could not go to the nearest bookshop and buy a copy. He had either to copy the text from another manuscript with his own hand, or to arrange for somebody to copy it for him.

Rich Romans, who no doubt would today be called publishers, employed slaves to do the copying *en masse*. Up to a hundred such scribes would sit and copy a book from the dictation of a fellow slave; that is to say they "worked by ear". In such a way up to a hundred copies of a popular book much in demand (a "best-seller" in our terms) could be made at one and the same time.

In the Middle Ages the method of multiplying ancient manuscripts was different. Copying was regarded as meritorious work in the eyes of monks, especially those of the Benedictine order, on a level with praying or tilling the soil. The monk sat in the scriptorium and wrote from a codex placed before him. These two forms of copying, by eye and by ear—that is to say, hearing a manuscript read and writing it down—led to two different types of mistakes, which occur in our manuscripts. Such errors were occasionally corrected, as far as possible, by special correctors in ancient times; but they sometimes still continued to plague the editors of ancient texts. Readings can be completely altered by the change of a letter or so, especially in Greek and Latin, and modern editors of ancient texts must not only be familiar with the form of ancient writing (the so-called paleography) but also ponder the possible variations from the original—hence many learned disputes. Not everyone can be as resolute as the French savant who ("by mistake", he said) poured ink over a disputed sentence in a unique manuscript, so that no one can now challenge his reading! If one copies a book from another manuscript by eye, it is of course a legible one, and the mistakes are subjective errors of vision. For instance, if a word occurs in one line and then is repeated two or three lines lower down, a careless scribe might "jump" with his eye from one to the other and omit several lines or even whole paragraphs in between. On the other hand, in the same way he may repeat the same passage twice.

Quite different are the errors of the ear, made by copyists to whom texts were read aloud. There in particular, words pronounced similarly could be confused, and one word written where another was meant. In both cases certain letters were particularly apt to be confused because they resembled each other—for instance in the square Hebrew script the R and the D, resh and daleth, which are very similar and easily confused, although more so by the eye-copyist. The correction of these mistakes, of course, is a special science, the science of the editing and amending of ancient texts.

2. Correcting Manuscripts

The correction of the ancient manuscripts, whether undertaken by a corrector on the spot or by a later owner of the manuscript, could be done in several ways. The mistake could be struck out and the correct version written above it, or it could be corrected on the spot by scratching or washing out the word which contained the mistake and writing the new one over it. From the point of view of the modern editor the first method is of course greatly preferable, because it gives both versions with no need for guessing. In the case of the Bible, the text of which was always treated with special respect by the Jews, there was a whole school of "Men of Tradition" or Massoretes who from the 7th century onwards worked on establishing a "correct" text. The discussion of which books were "canoni-

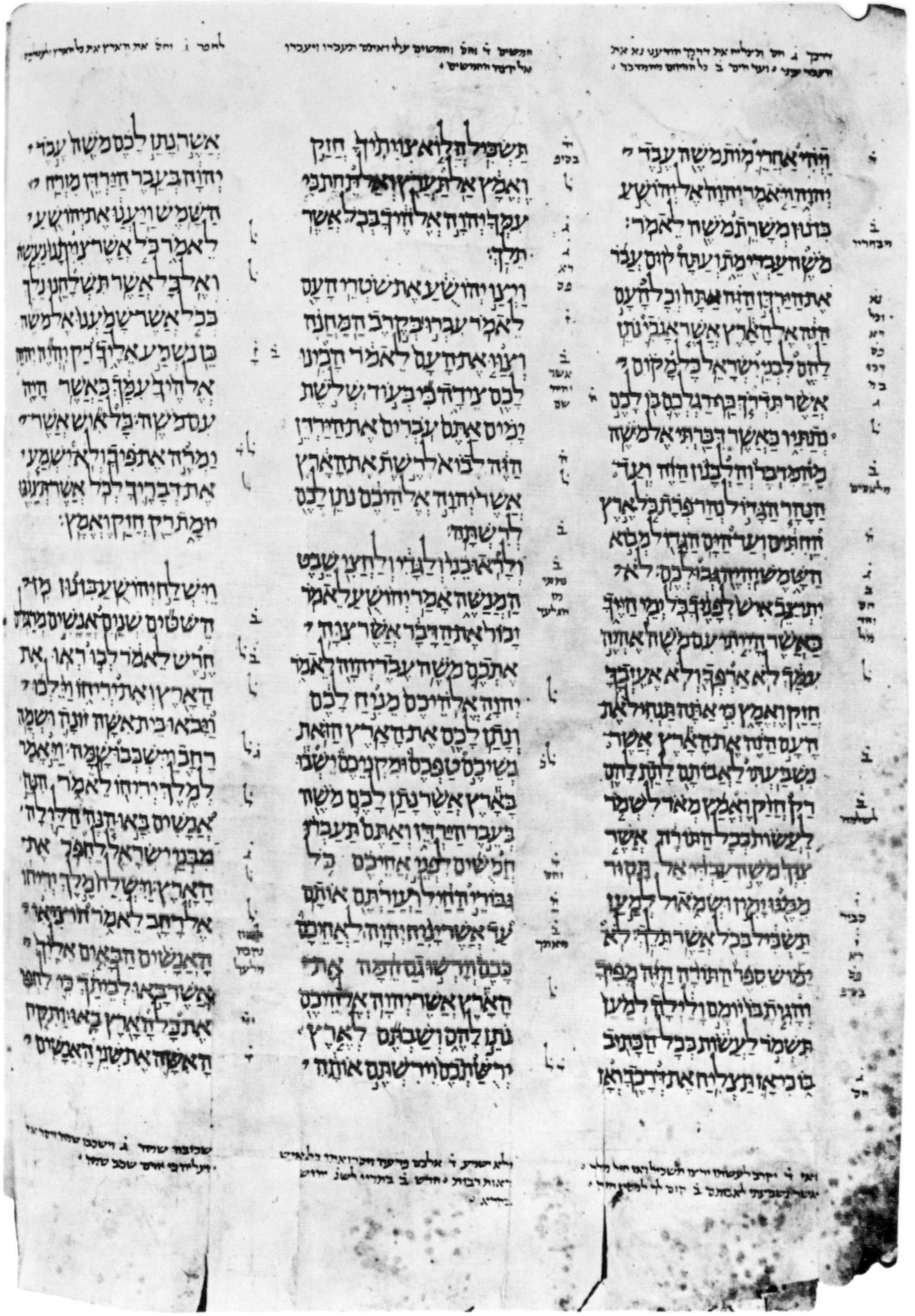

Part of a Bible manuscript showing Masoretic script

A Jewish scribe writing a Torah scroll

cal' and hence part of the Bible began as early as the 2nd century and still continues. The Massoretes were mainly engaged in providing the original, purely consonantal text (usual in early semitic writing) with vowels, so as to make pronunciation standard. They then counted the number of words in each book of the Bible, and the number of its verses, and marked the middle word in each book. During their work, the Massoretes noted in the "received text" between 1,400 and 1,500 verses where they believed a textual error had crept into the Holy Scriptures. But they dared not make corrections in the body of the text; instead they noted in the margin what they considered to have been the correct word. In this way they created a difference between

what in Hebrew is called the *qeri*, the way the word should be read (the correct way), and the *ketib*, what was written in the text of the Bible scroll.

3. Bible Manuscripts

The preparation of Bible manuscripts, especially that of the scrolls of the Torah used in the synagogues, is a very complicated process; they are produced with very great care. Instructions have been laid down, prescribing the materials from which the rolls should be made, how the sheets should be fastened, the composition of the ink to be used, the careful marking of lines on the manuscript before a single word is written, the number of letters in each line, the number of columns in each scroll, and so on. It is forbidden for a scribe to copy the text from memory; he has to use another scroll and refer to it for each word. Space between letters has to be a hair's breadth, and that between words the breadth of a narrow letter. The scribe has to take a ritual bath before starting to write, so as to purify himself. He is enjoined to take care of his pen and ink, and especially not to write the four-letter name of God (the *tetragrammaton*) with a pen freshly dipped in ink, lest he make a blot. And while writing he has to rid his mind of extraneous thoughts, and so concentrate all his faculties upon the task before him that: "even if he were spoken to by a king he should not answer".

Of course these rules, which were applied to the Bible scriptural texts, were not always followed in the case of secular literature. However, the Greek critics of the Hellenistic period treated the text of Homer more or less the way in which the Jews treated their Bible. The number of lines in each book were counted, and special signs were devised to mark lines which were considered spurious or corrupt. Like their Jewish colleagues the Massoretes, the Greek textual critics did not dare to interfere with the text itself, which was first written down in the time of Peisistratos of Athens in the 6th century BC; but they could and did mark lines in the margin.

Overleaf right:
Jewish gilt glass plates, 4th century. Note the ark containing scrolls.

Right: *Sephardic Torah scroll*

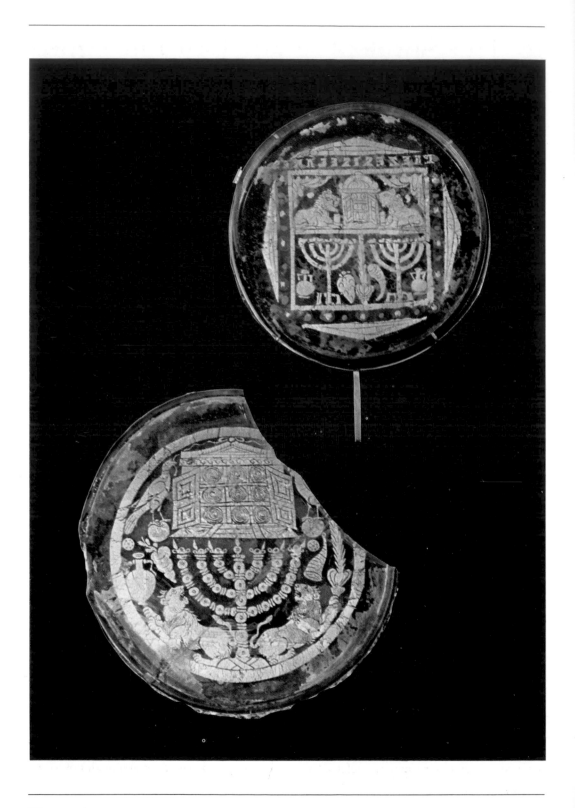

IV The Survival of Ancient Literature

Almost all ancient classical literature was written on parchment; but as always in the case of books copied by hand, there was a danger that only a single copy of the work would remain; and if that one were to be destroyed the whole work would be lost to posterity. The preservation and subsequent printing of the manuscripts of antiquity saved these works from oblivion —this was the great achievement of the copyists and scholars of the Middle Ages. They did not preserve the whole of the extant literature, but worked selectively; the principles of selection on which they operated will be discussed later. We may only note with regret that no more than about 10 per cent of the ancient Greek literature has been preserved, and only about one-third of the Latin. This shows the dangers inherent in the use of manuscript as opposed to printing.

1. Greek and Latin Literature

While we may deeply regret what has been lost of Latin and, especially, Greek literature, we might at the same time remember with gratitude those devoted scribes of the Middle Ages, who were instrumental in preserving the little we have. In this matter we must make a distinction between Greek and Latin literature, a distinction which finds expression in the relative survival percentage referred to above. Greek was practically unknown to the copyists of Medieval Europe. A standard phrase used by the monks in various monasteries of Western Europe, which they wrote down in copying mixed manuscripts, was *Graeca sunt, non leguntur*, meaning "these words are in Greek so they cannot be read". The Byzantines, on the other hand, who preserved the classical Greek tradition and the Greek language, were constantly copying and re-copying the texts in their possession throughout the Middle Ages, till the fall of Constantinople in 1453 AD. Unfortunately their selection of texts was very much restricted. Even by this early stage, only those texts had survived which had been used in schools, where they were regarded as models of pure diction.

From the Attic prose writers there remained the works of Thucydides and Plato, and selected plays of the classical triad of Greek tragedians, Aeschylus, Sophocles, Euripides; and the writer of comedies, Aristophanes. To realize the narrowness of this selection it is enough to remember that out of 90 plays written by Aristophanes, only 11 have survived, because these were used as school texts. The extant manuscripts with their numerous glosses, which explain the terms used, survive until today. Any author not regarded as an approved classic, or any work not toeing the line of what the later grammarians regarded as pure Greek, was soon lost and forgotten.

2. Byzantine Compilations

On the other hand the Byzantines still possessed a great deal of technical literature, including treatises on all sorts of subjects from strategy to cookery. But these too became superseded in the 9th century by digests. For convenience, and in a spirit of misguided diligence, certain authors began to prepare encyclopedias of excerpts - what we might call the "Reader's Digests" of the time; but instead of helping the better understanding and larger distribution of the originals "digested", such compilations turned out to be the ruin of the primary material. For instance the patriarch Photius of Constantinople, who lived in the middle of the 9th century, compiled an enormous work which he called *Bibliotheca*. In it he excerpted 280 codices of various historians. Of course, once these excerpts were readily available, readers began to neglect the original books and these were soon lost. The same effect was produced by another of Photius' works, his *Lexicon*. After Photius came a royal "digester", the Emperor Constantine VII, called Porphyrogenetos ("born in the purple") because he was born in the Purple Chamber of the palace at Constantinople, where children of reigning emperors first saw the light of day. Constantine VII lived in the first half of the 10th century. By his orders encyclopedias were compiled on history (under 53 headings), giving excerpts from many ancient historians. Again, once the excerpts were made, the originals were threatened. Other Byzantine encyclopedias dealt with agriculture and medicine, and again brought about the loss of the original works.

3. Greek Anthology

One exception from this general rule over which we must certainly rejoice is the *Greek Anthology*. This is a collection of short poems based on several anthologies (*Garlands*, as they were called). The first of these "garlands of poetic flowers" was made by Menander, the Greek poet of Gadara (in Transjordan) as early as the 1st century BC. This garland, and a few other later ones, were all copied together by a Byzantine visitor named Cephalas, about AD 970. The manuscript copy which survived was written in the 11th century. After many vicissitudes it came in the 16th century into the possession of the Elector Palatine, a German prince who lived in Heidelberg on the Rhine, and it became known as the "Palatine Anthology". In 1623, during the Thirty Years' War, when the army of the Catholic League under Tilly plundered Heidelberg, the manuscript (with many others) was presented by the conqueror to the Vatican library. There it remained till the time of Napoleon. In 1797 it was taken to Paris and became part of the Musee Napoleon, the great mass of works of art and antiquities compiled into a great European collection by order of the emperor. After 1815, as part of the reparations after Waterloo, books 1-12 of the Palatine Anthology were returned to Heidelberg, where they still are today, and 48 leaves remained in Paris.

4. The Destruction of Manuscripts

This is only one example of the great wanderings of the famous Greek manuscripts from one collection and country to another. Interest in Greek manuscripts revived in Western Europe for a short time at the time of the Crusades in the 12th century. There were always some soldiers ready to plunder, and collectors or scholars willing to buy the loot. When the Normans took Saloniki in 1185, they sold books by shiploads to the Italians, who were already interested in them at least as merchandise. Some such manuscripts fared badly later on in Europe. For instance, after the sack of Constantinople in 1204 a copy of one of Aristotle's works was brought to Paris where it was burnt because it expressed heretical opinions. Many precious works vanished in such a way; book-burning, the favourite game of fanatics of all sorts, is comparatively innocuous when played with printed works, because there are usually enough copies left; but it can be disastrous with manuscripts. It is said that at the time of the conquest of Constantinople by the Crusaders in 1204 an enormous number of books—about 120,000 volumes—were destroyed by the ignorant conquerors. Of course there were earlier cases of similar destruction: 400,000 volumes were lost when the great library of Alexandria was partly burnt during the fighting between Caesar (allied with Cleopatra) and the Egyptians in 48 BC; this loss was probably replaced in the later peaceful times of Roman rule.

5. The Survival of Latin Literature

Matters were different in the West as far as Latin was concerned. Throughout the Middle Ages the language of the Romans was widely understood, at least by churchmen, and occasionally the monks even copied authors who were not of direct interest to the Church. Centres of learning were established in the depths of the Dark Ages by the Irish monk Columba, who set up his monastery at Bobbio in Italy in the 7th century. There at his behest copyists reproduced a considerable quantity of manuscripts of the ancient authors.

In the eyes of the Benedictine monks, the copying of manuscripts was a work acceptable to God, as good as or perhaps even better than cultivating the land or planting vines. In consequence the monks divided their time between prayer, sleep, work in the fields and copying. In the 9th century, for instance, Servatius Lupus, who was Abbott at Ferrieres in France, collected a good library; for like many bibliophiles in later ages, he was an eager borrower and a wary lender of books. He was always ready to borrow from others in order to have as many manuscripts copied as possible, but was very, very careful when it came to passing on books from his own collection for copying. In many monasteries at that time special officers were appointed in charge of the copyists. Great care was taken under the Benedictine rules that the copying should be careful and exact. A librarian, or *armarius* (from *armorium*, a cupboard, *armoire* in French) was in charge of the manuscript collection.

Deep silence was observed in the libraries of the monastic orders. In some, borrowers therefore developed a special sign language.

If they made a sign as if to turn the pages of a book, it meant they wanted books, and special signs were then used to indicate different kinds of books. If one wanted a manuscript of the Psalms, hands were held over the head, as a sign of the crown of David, the royal psalmist. If, however (God forbid), one wanted a copy by an author who was not approved by the Church—a pagan author, for instance—the sign was to scratch behind the ear after the manner of the dog, indicating contempt for this kind of work.

One difficulty which plagued those in charge of the copying in the monasteries of old was that good parchment became rarer and rarer in Europe. Hence the monks, who had also to provide the books to be used in prayers, were often tempted to erase an old text — which could be done easily with a sponge—and to write another one over it. Thus a prayer book, a book of Psalms, or a theological work which was needed urgently was written in bold black Gothic script over the faded lines of an ancient author, infinitely more precious in our eyes. Such manuscripts, which are called *palimpsests*, can often deliver the secrets of the erased writings to a careful student, especially nowadays, by the use of scientific devices such as infra-red rays. Then the erased part under the later writing appears as if by magic and can be read. The works of several ancient authors, lawyers and orators were recovered in this way. It is only very exceptionally that we find the process reversed and, for instance, a translation of the Iliad written over a copy of the Epistles of St. Paul.

The great monastery libraries of the Middle Ages were those of St. Gallen in Switzerland, of the 11th or 12th century, where over 1,000 volumes were collected, and Monte Cassino, a Benedictine monastery in Italy

A page from the Northumbrian Bible depicting Ezra the Scribe

which again became famous at the time of the Second World War. There, at the end of the 11th century, an Abbot, who later became Pope Victor II, had many pagan authors—Latin ones, of course—copied for his library.

One of the most popular of these ancient authors was Virgil, because he was regarded as one of the prophets who had foretold the coming of Christ. This mistaken assumption was based on his gloweringly "prophetic" words describing Aeneas' vision of the unborn souls, including that of Marcellus, a descendant of the Emperor Augustus (the patron of Virgil). Marcellus died young, but while he was still alive Virgil prophesied for him a splendid future. Virgil was regarded as a prophet and in some more popular legends also as a sorcerer. His texts were used as oracles: people who wanted to know about their future stuck a needle into the text of the Aeneid or another of Virgil's poems; having stopped at a certain depth, they then opened the book at that page and looked up what the text said. As a result many of the ancient manuscripts of Virgil resemble sieves.

In general, apart from the most common texts in use, such as treatises on grammar or other schoolbooks, it is astonishing how few manuscripts have sufficed to preserve the best writers of antiquity. Of Petronius' Satyricon, for instance, there exist only one manuscript and a few isolated pages. Even Tacitus, the greatest of the Roman historians, has survived in but a handful of manuscripts, one in the Florentine library, and another in Paris; even so quite a substantial part of his work is lost. It is interesting to note that as late as 1902 an unknown manuscript of Tacitus turned up in a private library at Gesi, near Ancona in Italy. So hope need not be lost for future discoveries.

6. The Search for Ancient Literature

The revival of antiquarianism which took place about the beginning of the 14th century, the time of the forerunners of the Renaissance in Italy, has greatly affected our knowledge of ancient literature. Amongst the pioneers in this respect was the great Italian poet Petrarch, who lived from 1304-74. Petrarch looked all his life for manuscripts. He was overwhelmed when he found two unknown speeches by Cicero at Liège in Belgium in 1333. In 1345 he had the supreme happiness of finding a copy of the letters of Cicero; he copied out the whole manuscript in his own hand and even composed a "letter" to Cicero, telling his ghost that the letters had been found. But unfortunately Petrarch, who was in love with all antiquity, including the Greeks, did not himself know any Greek. In 1354 he was presented with a manuscript of Homer in the original, but it remained a closed book to him.

A second Italian, famous for quite another reason, who also continued the tradition of Petrarch was Bocaccio (1313-75). Bocaccio, today principally remembered as the author of the *Decamerone* and perhaps more famous for his naughty stories than for his serious learning, was a scholar in his own right. He collected quite a lot of manuscripts. He at least learnt Greek, and was able to use the manuscripts he acquired. By his time the splendid old libraries of the Middle Ages had fallen into sad decay; Bocaccio tells how when he visited the monastery of Monte Cassino and asked to see the famous library the monks just showed him the direction and said, "Go up if you like, nobody ever goes there." In a big room full of books and dust, he found manuscripts with handfuls of leaves torn out by the ignorant monks, who made them into Psalters and sold them for a few pennies to the public. They cut off strips from the margins of the old manuscripts in order to sell them as amulets to superstitious women. Bocaccio recovered in this library parts of the *Histories* and the *Annals* of Tacitus; these manuscripts are now in the Laurentine library in Florence, together with many others collected by zealous humanists under the patronage of the enlightened

Lucas sirus natōne anthiocensis arte medic9 discipulus apostoloȝ postea paulū secut9 uſȝ ad confessionē tu seruiens dño sine crimine: nuam netȝ uxorem unȝ habuit netȝ filios: septuaginta et quatuor annoȝ obiit in bithinia pleꝰ spiritu sancto. Qui cū iam scripta essent euāgelia p matheū quidē in iudea y marcū aut in italia: sancto instigante spiritu in achaie partibȝ hȝc scripsit euangeliū: significans etiā ipe in principio ante sui alia esse descripta. Cui extra ea ȝ ordo euāgelice dispositionis exposcita maxime necessitas laboris fuit: ut primū grecis fidelibȝ omni ꝓphetatione uenturi in carne dei cristi manifestata humanitate ne iudaicis fabulis attenti: in solo legis desiderio teneretur: uel ne hereticis fabulis et stultis solicitationibȝ seducti exciderent a ueritate elaboraret: dehinc ut in principio euangelij iohānis natiuitate presumpta cui euangelium scriberet et in quo electꝰ scriberet indicaret: cōtestās i se cōpleta esse ȝ essent ab alijs inchata. Cui ideo post baptismū filij dei a pfectione generationis i cristo implere repetēde a principio natiuitatis humane potestas ꝓmissa ē: ut requirentibȝ demonstraret in quo apprehendēs erat per nathan filiū dauid introitu recurrentis i deū generationis admisso indisparabilis dri ꝓdicās in hominibus cristū suū ꝓfecti opus hois redire in se p filiū faceret: qui per dauid patre uenientibus iter ꝓbebat in cristo. Cui luce non immerito etiā scribēdorum actuū apostoloȝ potestas i ministerio datur: ut deo in deū pleno et filio ꝓditionis extincto oratōe ab apostolis

facta sorte domini electionis numero compleretur: sitȝ paulus cōsummatione apostolicis actibȝ darer quē diu cōtra stimulū recalcitrante dñs elegiset. Quod et legentibȝ ac requirentibȝ deū et si per singula expediri a nobis utile fuerat: sciens tamē ȝ operātem agricolā oporteat de suis fructibus edere vitauimus publicā curiositatem: ne nō tā uolentibȝ deū demonstrare uideremur quā fastidientibus prodidisse. Explicit pfacio Incipit euangelium secundum lucam: Prohemium ꝓsius beati luce in euangelium finim

Quoniā quidē multi conati sunt ordinare narratiōnes ȝ i nobis complete sut rex sicut tradidrūt nobis ȝ ab inicio ipi uiderūt et ministri fuerūt sermonis: uisū ē et michi assecuto omnia a pricipio diligēter te ordie tibi scribere optie theophile: ut cognoscas coȝ uerboȝ de ȝbȝ eruditꝰ es ueritatē. Ι. Fuit in diebus herodis regis iudee sacerdos quidam nomine zacharias de uice abia: et uxor illi de filiabus aaron: et nomen eius elizabeth. Erant autem iusti ambo ante deum: incedentes in omnibus mandatis et iustificationibus domini sine querela. Et non erat illis filius eo ȝ esset elizabeth sterilis: et ambo processissent i diebȝ suis. Factū est aut cū sacerdotio fungeretur zacharias in ordine uicis sue ante deū: scdm cōsuetudinem sacerdotij sorte exijt ut incensum poneret ingressus in templū domini. Et omnis multitudo ppli erat orās foris hora incensi. Apparuit autem illi angelus dñi stans a dextris altaris

Meyers Konv.-Lexikon, 5. Aufl. Bibliographisches Institut in Leipzig.

Medici family.

The same sad story is told by another Italian humanist, a man slightly younger than Bocaccio, Poggio Bracciolini (1380-1459). As representative of an enlightened Renaissance Pope, Poggio made a systematic hunt through the monasteries of Northern Europe for manuscripts of ancient writers. He tells how he visited the formerly splendid monastery of St. Gallen and found the library, in one of the towers of the abbey, full of dust and darkness. But his dusty haul was a splendid one: it included Quintilian's *Institutio oratoria*, and works by the Roman poet Lucretius whose writings had been quite unknown till then. In 1421 Poggio found an old chest of manuscripts of Cicero in the Abbey of Monzo. He suffered the usual disappointments which attended other searchers for manuscripts —for instance he was told that there was a complete Pliny in one place, but this turned out to be a false lead.

One important turning-point in the knowledge of Greek literature in the West was the fall of Constantinople to the Ottoman Turks in 1453. Refugees from the imperial city escaped to Europe, and especially to Venice. They brought with them not only the knowledge of the Greek language, which they were able to disseminate by teaching Greek at the various universities, but also manuscripts by which the libraries of Europe were greatly enriched. Even before 1453 there had been Venetian embassies to Constantinople, who were told to collect all the manuscripts available.

At the end of the 15th century printing on paper revolutionized the whole problem of the survival of ancient literature. Of course matters did not go altogether smoothly; as with every revolution in human knowledge, there was a good deal of resistance to this new-fangled method, however much the old printers tried to imitate the hand-written manuscripts. One of the first of the booksellers and book traders of the Renaissance, Vespasiano da Portici, engaged 45 copyists to prepare a library at San Lorenzo for one of the Medicis; they wrote 200 manuscripts in two years. Da Portici produced in 14 years a whole library for the Duke of Urbino in Italy, "beautiful volumes all bound in crimson and silver and all," as he says, "written with the pen, for the Duke would be ashamed to possess a single printed book."

Nevertheless, the future was with the new medium. Two Germans who worked with Fust, the companion of Gutenberg in Mainz, established the first press in Italy at Subiaco and in 1465 printed the first Latin book, Cicero's *De Oratore*. The Greek text of Homer was first printed at Florence in 1488; the fables of Aesop even earlier in 1478. The first printers had to cut special type, imitating the normal Byzantine manuscripts of their times, to print their *incunabula*. The greatest of the early presses, that of Aldus Manutius, was established in Venice; from 1449 to 1515 he published all the Greek manuscripts which were then available. From that time onwards the classics have been on record in thousands of copies, and we may hope that whatever future disasters may strike humanity, this heritage will not be lost again, as happened to such a ruinous extent at the end of antiquity.

Left: *A page from the Gutenberg Bible*

A scene from the Book of the Dead showing the weighing of the soul

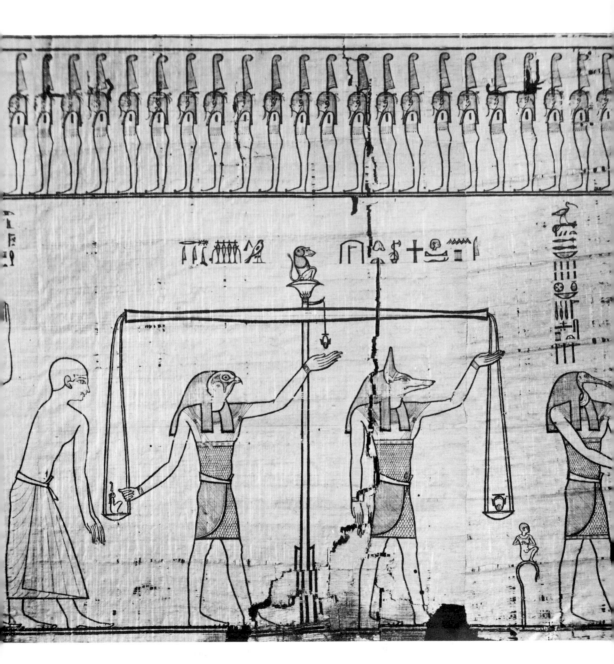

V Illustrated Manuscripts

The idea of "illuminating" (illustrating) a text with pictures originated, it seems, in Egypt, where the hieroglyphic writing, in itself a kind of pictorial script, blended easily with visual reflections of the literary text. The drawings of the images and/or symbols of the gods were certainly regarded as possessing a magical power, an idea going back to primitive mentality. Accordingly, to draw a picture of a person was equivalent to acquiring a magic power over his acts. Hence we may assume that in the earliest illustrated texts extant, the copies of the "Book of the Dead", pictures and text were regarded as of equal importance. This book was in fact a guide to the Nether World put into the tomb in order to enable the deceased to give the correct answers when examined about his deeds by the dread judges of his soul, and to teach him how to go from one place to another in the world below. This continuous narrative probably served as the basis for the general conception of sub-dividing of the action in a story into single acts, to each of which a separate visual expression was given. The main characters are of course shown again and again in each of the pictures, only the minor personages and the background changed according to the circumstances.

Possibly the Greeks became acquainted with the Egyptian illustrated papyri in the Hellenistic period, when they came to rule over Egypt. But even before that the narrative approach and the sub-division of a story with the identical hero in various episodes can be seen in representations of the Labours of Hercules or Theseus in architectural sculpture. One of the earliest illustrated Greek manuscripts, a papyrus containing the story of the Labours of Hercules, shows his encounter with the Nemean lion in three separate pictures: the meeting, the fight and the victory.

Another type of illustration can be found in the ancient treatises on technical matters, such as the work of Dioscorides —manuals of Botany or Zoology certainly gained enormously by having pictures of the plants or beasts to amplify the verbal descriptions. The same is true of medical works and other compositions of similar character.

The illustrated Iliad might well go back to the Hellenistic period—although the earliest *extant* manuscript with illustrations, the "Ilias Ambrosiana", is a codex of the 4th century AD—as is another famous illuminated classical text, the Vatican Virgil.

1. Book Illustration

This way of visualizing the Greek "Bible" was in all probability the inspiration for the

ΑΠΟΓΗΣΕΠΙΘΑΜΙΑΙΟΥΣ
ΤΙΚΑΙΜΕΤΥΟΝΑΣΡΙΖΑΝ
ΠΑΡΑΠΛΗΣΙΑΝΤΗΙΟ
ΖΜΥΡΣΙΝΗΜΕΙΖΟ
ΝΑΔΕΚΑΙΕΥΧΔΗΚΑ
ωΤΕΡΑΝ·ΦΥΕΤΑΙΕΝ
ΤΟΠΟΙΣΟΡΙΝΟΙΣ·ΔΥΝΑ
ΜΙΝΑΣΕΧΕΙΗΡΙΖΑΠΙ
ΝΟΜΕΝΗΠΑΡΑΧΜω
ΕΣΠΛΗΘΟΣΜΕΤΑΟΙ
ΝΟΥΓΛΥΚΕΟΣ·ΒΟΗ
ΘΕΙΝΤΑΙΣΔΥΣΤΟΚΟΥ
ΣΑΙΣΚΑΙΣΤΡΑΓΓΟΥ
ΡΙωΣΙΝ·ΑΠΕΙΔΑΣΚΑΙΑΙΜΑ
ΔΑΦΝΟΕΙΔΕΣ·ΟΙΔΕΣΥΠΕ
ΧΙΤΑΛΟΝ·ΟΙΔΕΧΑΜΑΙΔΑ
ΦΝΗΗΓΟΙΔΕΠΕΠΛΟΝ
ΚΑΛΟΥΣΙ·ΘΑΜΝΙΣΚΟΣ
ΕΣΤΙΓΙΠΗΧΕωΣΤΟΥΦΟΣ
ΕΧωΝΚΛΑΔΟΥΣΠΟΛΛΟΥΣ
ΚΑΙΛΕΠΤΟΥΔΕΙΣΠΡΟΣ
ΤωΑΝωΘΕΝΗΜΙΣΕΙ
ΕΡΥΛΛΟΦΟΡΟΥΣ·ΕΡΛΟΙ
ΔΕΛΣΠΕΡΙΤΑΣΡΑΒΔΟΥΣ
ΧΛΙΣΧΡΟΣ·ΙΣΧΥΡΟΣ·ΦΥΛ
ΛΑΔΑΦΝΗΣΕΟΙΚΟΤΑ·
ΜΑΛΑΚωΤΕΡΑΔΕΚΑΙ
ΧΥΡωΤΕΡΑ·ΟΥΚΕΥΚΛΑ
ΣΤΑΔΑΚΝΟΝΤΑΚΑΙΠΥ
ΡΟΥΝΤΑΤΟΣΤΟΜΑΚΑΙΦΑΡΥΓΓΑ·ΑΝΘΗΛΕΥ
ΙΚΑΚΑΡΠΟΝΔΕΜΕΛΑΝΑΟΤΑΝΠΕΠΑΝΘΗΙ·
ΡΙΖΑΑΧΡΕΙΟΣ·ΦΥΕΤΑΙΕΝΟΡΙΝΟΙΣΤΟΠΟΙΣ·
ΛΑΓΙΣΔΕΤΟΦΥΛΛΟΝΑΥΤΟΥΞΗΡΟΝΠΙΝΕ
ΑΡΟΝΠΟΘΕΝΚΑΤΑΚΟΙΛΙΑΝΦΛΕΓΜΑΤω
ΔΗ·ΚΙΝΕΙΚΑΙΕΜΕΤΟΥΣ·ΚΑΙΕΜΜΗΝΑ

Battle scenes from the Ambrosian Iliad

Left: *A Greek zoological text*

Fragment of the Ambrosian Iliad: Aphrodite shows Zeus her hand.

The Ambrosian Iliad. The Greeks draw their boats to the sea.

Iliad illustration showing Briseis being taken away by the herald

Bible illustrations. The latter were probably conceived at Alexandria, the focus of Hellenistic Judaism, as part of the effort then made by Philo and his aide to bring the Gentiles nearer to Judaism within Greek culture. For this purpose the Bible story was given a Greek literary form, epic or dramatic as the case may be. Parallel to the literary effort went the visual one—the biblical events were given the form, familiar to the educated Greek, of a mythological story. For instance the imagery of the story of the Creation was modelled on the myth of Prometheus, that of Adam and Eve on Jason and Medea (with the snake replacing the legendary dragon), that of Jonah on Endymion, etc. The reflection of this illustrative approach can still be found in the frescoes of the synagogue at Dura-Europos (3rd century AD), in the paintings of the early Christian catacombs, the wall mosaics of the early churches such as Santa Maria Maggiore in Rome, and in synagogue floor mosaics such as Beth Alpha, Gerasa and Naaran.

2. Illustrated Manuscripts of the Bible

Of illustrated Bible manuscripts proper none that has survived is earlier than the 6th century (the Vienna Genesis); others (the Joshua Roll and the Octateuches, meaning the Pentateuch to Kings) are much later. All these (except the Joshua Roll) are codices, and hence represent the later stage of the illustrative process. The illustrators of a papyrus scroll could insert a picture in every column, that is to say, they could give an image to every 30 to 40 lines of text. On the other hand such a lavish use of illustrations was permissible in the codices only in the most sumptuous copies, such as the Vienna Genesis, written and drawn on purple leaves. Even then, although a picture occurs on every page, and the text was written below, the illustrations had often to be compressed by showing one or two events together on one page; otherwise the illustrations would have outrun the text. For example, we have Joseph and Potiphar's wife on one and the same page, with Joseph being accused before Potiphar on the lower part. Often the arrangement of the illustrations in two tiers gives a most artistic effect, as for instance

Mosaic floor of the ancient Beth Alpha Synagogue: the sun in its chariot with four horses and the Zodiac panel

when Jacob and his family cross a bridge which divides the picture in two. In certain manuscripts, such as the Paris Psalter, one page was given to every detail of the story, such as David the shepherd and his anointment by Samuel or Hezekiah's prayer and its fulfillment. But even there David's fight with Goliath and his victory are represented together with the appropriate personifications, "Fortitude" with David and "Impudence" with Goliath.

The original iconographic tradition of these illustrations was essentially Hellenistic. However, as time went on only the main figures kept their original garb while most of the others were represented in contemporary costume. Thus in the Vienna Genesis Pharaoh is a Byzantine emperor, Potiphar a Byzantine

The combat between David and Goliath (Paris Psalter, 11th century) - David is supported by "Fortitude" and Goliath by "Impudence".

court official, etcetera, whereas in the Paris Psalter David is anointed King in the Germanic manner by being lifted on a shield by his followers.

The original illustrations were evidently conceived for some sort of paraphrase of the biblical stories, for even in the eyes of the Hellenized Jews *Septuagint* text was much too holy to be "desecrated" by pictures, a restriction which applied *a fortiori* to the Hebrew original. Later, Christian illuminators borrowed the Judaeo-Hellenistic concept, but did not feel bound to refrain from illustrating the Greek Septuagint or the Latin Vulgate respectively. They used the full text of the Scriptures, selecting suitable episodes for illumination. In one detail, however, the original Jewish conception remained valid till the 11th century at least: God is never represented as a person. His power is symbolized even in Christian manuscripts, as in Jewish mosaics or frescoes, by the outstretched hand, and nothing more.

On the whole the early illuminated manuscripts are certainly one of the most interesting and aesthetically pleasing forms of ancient art.

Samuel anoints David. Illuminated Bible, Venice

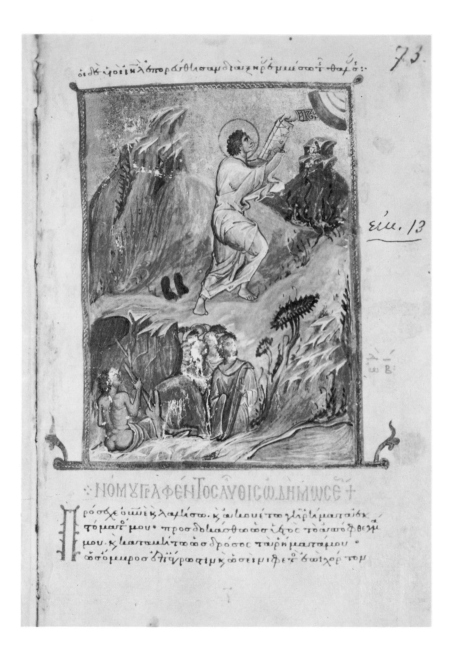

A page from Psalter and New Testament showing Moses receiving the Law. Constantinople, about 1083 A.D.

Jesus entering Jerusalem on Palm Sunday. From an ancient Christian manuscript

VI Jewish Manuscripts

Jewish literature in the Greek language was very plentiful in the Hellenistic and Roman period. With the gradual widening of the chasm between the Jewish and Greco-Roman cultures which followed upon the two Jewish wars against Rome and the destruction of the Temple, the "Books of the Heretics"—*Minim,* those of a different kind *(min)* to the majority of the Jewish nation—became forbidden and were liable to destruction. Hence the whole edifice of Judeo-Greek literature collapsed into oblivion.

Only the works of those writers who happened to have some connection with Christianity were preserved. These included, for instance, those of Philo, the philosopher of Alexandria, who used the allegorical explanation of the Bible, which once suited the point of view and arguments of early Christianity. Another of the authors rescued from burning was Josephus. In his works there was an interpolated passage about Jesus Christ, used by Christian propagandists as "proof" of the existence of Jesus (the genuine wording of this passage has recently been unearthed in an Arabic polemical work against Christians).

Moreover, Josephus' description of the terrors of the siege and the ultimate destruction of the Jerusalem site of the Second Temple seemed to suit the prophecies written down in the name of Jesus. These authors were preserved together with the Books of the Maccabees as canonized. The latter were regarded as part of the scriptures and joined to the manuscript of the Septuagint. We thus owe to the Christian church almost all our real knowledge of the history of the Second Temple.

1. The Hebrew Bible Manuscripts

The manuscripts of the Bible of course had a different fate. They were carefully copied after the rules of the Massoretes. Even biblical texts and scraps of them were carefully preserved, for instance the Nash papyrus which contains the earliest extant version of the Ten Commandments. It dates to the 2nd century BC and hence was the oldest part of the Bible known to exist before the discovery of the Dead Sea Scrolls. After it and a few more scraps of manuscripts there comes an enor-

The Nash papyrus containing the Ten Commandments, 2nd century BC

mous gap in our knowledge of biblical texts. The complete copies of the Hebrew Bible, preserved in manuscripts of the 10th century in the Leningrad library in Russia and in the British Museum in London, are the earliest ones known, again before the finding of the

Detail of the Keter ha-Torah, the Aleppo Bible Manuscript, 9th-10th century

Scrolls. They represent the Massoretic tradition of the school of Tiberias, established by a family called Ben-Asher. To the same group of manuscripts belongs the famous *Keter ha-Torah*, the "Crown of the Law". Written by Aaron Ben-Asher at the end of the 9th or the beginning of the 10th century AD, it was kept for several centuries at the Aleppo synagogue in Syria. Many scholars tried to copy or photograph it, but in vain. In 1948, when the State of Israel was established, anti-Jewish riots broke out in Aleppo. The synagogue was burnt down by an Arab mob and it was believed that the *Keter ha-Torah* was burnt with it. Scholars the world over mourned the tragic and irretrievable loss of this ancient text. But luckily the manuscript was secretly almost completely saved, and carried to Israel, where it is at present being carefully guarded in Jerusalem. We shall discuss the biblical texts found at Qumran in Chapter VI (2).

2 . Codex Sinaiticus

The copies of the Greek translation of the Bible (the *Septuagint*) which was adopted by the Greek-speaking section of the Christian

Moses, Aaron and the elders. French manuscript miscellany, 13th century

"The Dayyenu" from a Spanish Haggadah of the 14th century

church are more numerous. As the Septuagint translation was made before the establishment of the Massoretic text, there are many differences between it and the Hebrew text of the Bible as we know it. The oldest complete manuscript of the *Septuagint* is the so-called *Codex Sinaiticus*; of earlier texts only parts of Deuteronomy have been preserved, dated to the 2nd century BC. They were acquired by the American collector Chester Beatty and were published by Sir Frederick Kenyon in 1930. A complete text of the Septuagint was prepared by the School of Caesarea, established by the Christian scholar Ongenes, who also studied the Hebrew text, and by his pupil Eusebius. The Codex Sinaiticus was discovered in the monastery of St. Catherine on Mount Sinai in 1844. Then a German biblical scholar called Tischendorf visited the monastery. He found that the monks had collected in a basket loose pages of a vellum manuscript, in order to use as fuel. Tischendorf noticed at once the beautiful Greek script of the 4th century. On being told that this was the next batch marked for the oven, he begged the monks to allow him to present a few leaves to his patron, the King of Saxony. They agreed, and Tischendorf came away with 43 leaves. On a later visit to the Near East (in 1859) he persuaded the monks to present the remaining parts of the same biblical manuscript to the Emperor of Russia. This part contained 199 leaves of the Old Testament, and the entire text of the New Testament, 347 leaves in all, written on the finest vellum. They remained in Russia till 1933, when the Codex Sinaiticus, as it became known, was sold to the British Museum for £100,000. Another Codex of the *Septuagint*, the Codex Alexandrinus (so called because it came from Alexandria), reached Britain in 1627 as a gift of the Patriarch of Constantinople to King Charles I. It too is in the British Museum. The third of the famous codices of the Septuagint is at the Vatican Library in Rome, where it has been since 1481 at least.

Reproduction from a handwritten illuminated minute Psalter. Parchment.
Lisbon workshop, last third of 15th century.

3. Post-Biblical Jewish Manuscripts

Let us now return to the rest of Jewish literature, in Hebrew or Aramaic. The Oral Law codified in the Mishna, and the Gemara, the extended commentary upon it, in its two versions (the smaller Palestinian one and the Babylonian), were for a long time committed entirely to memory and were not allowed to be written. This explains the many mnemonic arrangements found in their text, which were intended to facilitate remembering the Oral Law. The famous Rabbi Akiba, the foremost scholar of the 2nd century AD, seems to have written down at least some guiding details of the Mishna. His notes were used by the Patriarch Judah I (135-218) in editing the text of the Mishna as we know it. The manuscripts of the Mishna and the Talmud were diligently copied throughout the Middle Ages by scholars in all Jewish communities; and they were carefully kept. In fact, no writing in Hebrew letters could be thrown away under Jewish laws as it might contain the Divine name. Spoiled manuscripts were kept in special rooms near the synagogues, such a room being called a *Genizah*. The most famous of these storerooms is the *Genizah* of Cairo, once belonging to the ancient Jewish community of Fustat, which had existed there since the 10th century. Hundreds, perhaps even thousands, of fragments of manuscript texts, documents and letters were recovered from there by various scholars. The *Genizah* finds include, for instance, the lost Hebrew text of Ben Sirah (Eulenastes). Most of this collection has been brought to Oxford or New York, where the archives have been the happy hunting ground for scholars ever since.

As a people with literary leanings, the Jews were of course quite used to copying manuscripts for private or public use. From the Hellenistic period onwards every child, or at least every son, was taught to read and to write. But because of the difficulties of Jewish life in Medieval Europe, and the many persecutions which the Jews underwent — being chased from one country to another — the number of Hebrew manuscripts preserved is much less than we could reasonably expect. The alleged hostility to Christianity of the Talmud and the commentaries upon it, on which stress was so often laid by the Christian disputants with the Jews and more especially by renegade Jews, led to wholesale burning of Talmudic manuscripts. In consequence complete copies of the Talmuds, both the Babylonian and the "Jerusalem" (Palestinian), are exceedingly rare; there are only two or three of each of them in all. Many fragments of manuscripts, or scraps, were preserved here and there. Sometimes, paradoxically, the enemies of the Jews, who had confiscated manuscripts, and presented them to ecclesiastical libraries, were instrumental in their preservation.

In the end these found their way to libraries like the Vatican, or other public collections, where they could be studied at leisure.

Even the most complete Jewish manuscripts usually bear the marks of deletions or excisions. The Christian censors exercised their zeal against the manuscripts of the Talmud from an early period. Passages which were supposed to be hostile to Christianity, or insulting to Jesus and the apostles, were censored, but not always in a rational manner, the censors very often confusing the various meanings of the text, which they were unable to understand properly. Jews, on the other hand, prepared copies of the censored passages, which were kept in special notebooks; the lost passages can thus sometimes be restored.

With the printing of the earliest editions of the Talmud in the 15th century, the survival of the extant Jewish text was more or less assured, although there is an enormous amount of editing work to be done before it can be said that a critical copy of the rabbinical text exists.

VII The Search for Papyri

We now pass to another source of ancient writing, which has become increasingly important in the last century: *papyri*. It has already been explained that papyrus, a writing material made from reeds, was the most common "paper" of antiquity. This fact was gradually forgotten, because in the damp climate of almost all the countries of the Mediterranean (and certainly in all provinces of the Roman Empire in Western Europe) no papyri could survive, and in fact none were preserved except in the find at Herculaneum already mentioned, where preservation was due to quite exceptional circumstances; not in every place could one expect the convenient eruption of a volcano. However, in about the middle of the 19th century scholars noticed that in Egypt, wherever the Nile floodwaters did not penetrate, the dry desert climate constituted an excellent means of preserving all perishable materials including wood or papyrus. The cultivated areas of the Nile Valley dwindled considerably from the Hellenistic and Roman periods onwards till they reached their nadir in the 19th century, and extensive areas in which villages and towns had once existed had by then become deserts. The rubbish heaps of these ruins proved a fruitful source of material for antiquity dealers. The peasants working for them dug out any amount of papyri from such heaps. At first the value of this new material was hardly understood; we are told that sometimes the Arab dealers burnt the papyrus sheets to enjoy their aroma. However, step by step, scholars began to understand the value of this type of source. From 1870 the rubbish heaps of the Hellenistic towns and villages in the Faiyum became our main source of papyri. The discovery of the speeches of the Attic orator Hyperides (in 1887) was a surprise; although one speech, in which he had defended his mistress Phryne and obtained her acquittal by baring her to the jury, did not survive. In 1891 a short extract (probably a student's notes) of Aristotle's *Constitution of Athens* was discovered; also on a less elevated level the poems (Miambi) of one Herondas, texts of popular, not to say vulgar, nature, but very vivid indeed.

Systematic excavation for papyri was begun in 1895. Especially fruitful in this respect was the site of Oxyrrhynchus in the Faiyum where an enormous number of papyri were found. We learn from the excavators Greenfell and Hunt that in one heap the layers of papyrus were so thick that six pairs of men and boys had to work for several days to dig through them. The results of one day were 36 baskets of papyrus rolls; a further 25 baskets were collected on the next. Then came the discovery by Sir Flinders Petrie, made in his excavations of Gurob, that mummy cases, the Hellenistic substitute for the former mummy bindings of Egyptian times, were now made of papyrus sheets. And then in 1900 it was found that the mummies of crocodiles, the sacred animal of the Faiyum district, were also stuffed with papyrus. Although this was not always the case—in fact only two per cent of the crocodile mummies were thus treated—the consequences of this discovery were immense. Among the finds papyri of literary value began to turn up, the oldest one being a 4th century BC copy of the poet Timotheos. Shortly before the First World War Aramaic papyri were found in the Thebaid, first at Aswan and at Elephantine; the latter, an island also called Jeb in the Nile near Aswan.

The next texts threw a most important light on the life of the Jewish military colony settled at Elephantine by the Persians. They corresponded with the High Priest of Jerusalem and Sanballat the governor of Samaria. Another find of the same period was made at Avroman (Persia) in 1909. It produced papyri from a different region, one outside Egypt, and hence particularly interesting. In the middle of World War I (about 1915) there came to light the extensive archives of Zenon, an officer of Apollonius, the Minister of Finance of Ptolemy II of Egypt (middle of the 3rd century BC). Here were hundreds of papyri, letters received by Zenon, with his annotations and copies of letters sent by him, etcetera.

A letter from the Zenon archives, 3rd century BC

They throw a new light on the Ptolemaic administration of Egypt, especially from the economic side; some of the letters date from Zenon's visit to Palestine in 259 BC and are extremely valuable to us. They contain documentary evidence for the small principality which the Tobiad family had succeeded in establishing east of the Jordan in Ptolemaic times.

The search for papyri has continued systematically ever since. The excavations of Dura-Europos on the Euphrates have produced a lot of new materials, the more valuable because they are from a different milieu than the Egyptian one.

The literary value of the papyrus finds should not be underestimated. There are about 680 texts of Homer alone, 80 texts of Euripides, and other texts hitherto quite unknown, such as one complete play of the Attic comedian Menander (of whom we had previously heard only single sentences), and fairly substantial fragments of about six of his other plays. Papyri have of course been immensely valuable because of the light they have thrown on the history of Egypt in particular, and to a lesser extent on that of the other countries of the Near East. To quote but one example: the status of the Jews of Alexandria has been clarified by a copy of the letter of the Emperor Claudius to the community there concerning their rights of citizenship.

We know that in the great library of Alexandria there were once about 400,000 scrolls. Part of this collection was destroyed in the fighting between Julius Caesar and Cleopatra on one side and the Egyptian people on the other. The rest were burnt at a later period, possibly — according to one version—at the time of the Arab conquest. The light thrown by the papyri on the private lives, the economics, the law, the administrative arrangements and the religious life of the period is of enormous value to historians. Many facts recorded by ancient historians have been substantiated, sometimes in contradiction to later scholars'

theories. We must, however, remember two points as regards this material. The reading of the papyri is not always easy: the various clerks who wrote them were not always careful; writing as they were on business matters they were in a hurry, and instead of separating the letters of the Greek and Latin alphabets employed a running script which is sometimes very difficult to read. The other difficulty is the incomplete state of the preservation of most papyri. Archives have been dispersed, and sometimes parts of the same text were even purchased by different collections. The state of preservation of the manuscripts themselves is often very bad.

The second difficulty in evaluating the historical value of this material is that its distribution is very haphazard. Sometimes we know of the most minute administrative details, as in the case of certain districts of Roman or Ptolemaic Egypt which have been favoured by fate and were left lying high and dry. Many papyri finds made in such areas, and the Faiyum in particular, are hence overrated in historical perspective. Other districts along the desert fringe of Egypt are very fully documented; we know for instance that the village scribe of Cerceosivis in the 2nd century BC could not add correctly. On the other hand the royal capitals, Alexandria or Thebes, have left us no records; this is true of the whole Nile delta area, which was always being flooded and hence was too damp to preserve its papyri. As a result the information we have from this source is very one-sided; we must, so to speak, always lean backwards in estimating its general applicability.

1. Papyri Outside Egypt

Egypt was the driest of the ancient countries, and also the one in which papyrus was used most extensively of all. It is hence favoured in papyrology out of all proportion to its importance in antiquity. To sum up: the papyri thus form a most important source of knowledge about the ancient world, both for

Nessana papyrus containing a Greek glossary to Virgil's Aeneid

literary or technical books and for an image of everyday life. Papyrus, as we have seen, was the most common writing material of antiquity; it was still used by the Papal Chancellery in Rome in the 11th century. Gradually, however, because the material itself was no longer available in medieval Europe, the use of papyrus had to be given up even there. From the 12th century till the beginning of the excavation at Herculaneum in Italy in the 18th century, papyrus was practically unknown in Europe. At Herculaneum a whole library was discovered, but unfortunately it was in a very bad state. The hardening of the volcanic tufa and the seeping-in of seawater turned the papyri into carbonized lumps. Only by the use of special machines was it possible to detach single sheets, each of which had to be copied at once, before it fell into dust. The results were rather disappointing, as the library proved to have belonged to an adherent of the philosophy of Epinerus, and did not even contain the original works of the master but only some treatises of his pupils.

Only very recently has there been an opportunity to extend our knowledge of the written material outside Egypt; we have already mentioned those from Avroman and Dura-Europos. In Palestine finds of papyri were first made in the Negev at Nessana (Auja el Hafir) in 1935. The texts included a word-for-word translation of the Aeneid of Virgil into Greek. Obviously someone in Byzantine Nessana in the 6th century studied the Latin text of Virgil with the help of such a translation. The Nessana finds also included a number of documents of economic and literary character from the late Byzantine and early Arabic periods.

All the early finds were overshadowed by what has been described—with some exaggeration perhaps—as the greatest archaeological find of the century, the discovery of the scrolls near Khirbet Qumran not far from the shores of the Dead Sea. This discovery, made accidentally in 1947, has occupied the world of learning ever since, and we shall devote to it the last part of this book.

In the Arabic texts—mainly orders for delivery of wheat or requisition of guides sent by the Arab governors to the Byzantine clerks subordinate to them— we have some of the earliest specimens of Arabic writing, dating to a few decades after the Hijra. It is interesting incidentally to compare the bold strokes of the Arabic writing of the conquerors with the spidery writing of the Byzantines.

Besides their intrinsic importance, the Nessana texts also proved that papyri could be preserved outside Egypt and in other dry areas, for instance the desert surrounding the Dead Sea.

VIII The Dead Sea Scrolls

1. The History of the Scrolls

The valleys along the Dead Sea receive a very small amount of rainfall, only 80 mm a year; the deep beds of the valleys have been gouged out by water pouring down from the mountains. The numerous caves in the cliffs bordering on these valleys are quite dry enough to preserve perishable materials, such as wood, wool, textiles and papyri. Literary notices from the 3rd, 8th and later centuries record finds of ancient copies of the Bible in the vicinity of Jericho. These notices were not, however, taken particularly seriously until the famous discovery in 1947.

The story of the finding of the first scrolls in the vicinity of the Dead Sea is one of the romances of archaeology, which the public likes to devour but which occur, alas, only very rarely if at all in the life of the working archaeologist. A Bedouin shepherd boy, Muhammad edh-Dhib ("the Wolf"), was tending his goats in the vicinity of an old ruin known as Khirbet Qumran in the wilderness south-west of Jericho, not far from the Dead Sea shore. This site had been surveyed already in the seventies of the last century; it was regarded as a kind of Roman fort, a desert outpost. Climbing with his goats, Muhammad— at least so runs the tale— noticed a hole in the cliff opposite this ruin. He threw in a stone and heard the noise of breaking pottery. Intrigued by this, he and other members of his tribe entered the cave (Qumran Cave No. I) and found several jars full of rolls of parchment wrapped up in linen. The linen had been covered with pitch, and as a result the manuscripts had been fairly well preserved. Of course the Bedouins did not have the slightest idea about the nature of their find, or its importance, and so they consulted with one Kando, an antiquity dealer from Bethlehem, with whom they had some sort of commercial relationship. This man collected seven or eight of the scrolls found in Cave 1, and began to look for a purchaser, addressing himself to various people he knew in Jerusalem. Many of the scholars who were first confronted with the scrolls were entirely confused on seeing this material. It resembled nothing that they had known before; they tended to regard the whole thing as a forgery, a hoax, or in any case as something very strange. A few amongst them, including Professor Sukenik of the Hebrew University, recognized their antiquity. Sukenik succeeded in acquiring at least part of the find. The balance (save one roll which Kando kept hidden) was purchased by the Patriarch of the Syrian Uniate Community, Mar Samuel. The patriarch did not know the full value of his buy; but he consulted a scholar from the American School of Oriental Research in Jerusalem, allowing him to take photographs of the manuscripts. As a result copies of these texts, some of which were quite easily legible by any competent Hebraist, came into the hands of American scholars, in particular Professor. W. F. Albright, who at once recognized one of the manuscripts, the Isaiah Scroll I, to be the oldest manuscript of any book of the Bible, dating it back to the 2nd century BC—that is over one thousand years earlier than the earliest Bible manuscript previously known.

Finally, the four texts purchased by Mar Samuel were published in fascimile by Professor Millar Burrows and other American scholars. The four scrolls bought by Professor Sukenik were published after his death in 1955.

Unfortunately this important discovery was made on the eve of the end of the British Mandate, and of the Arab-Jewish War, which lasted from 1947 to 1948. It took, therefore, quite some time till scholars were able to approach the site of the find in order to start further research. Finally, an expedition from the French Biblical and Archaeological School in Jerusalem, led by Father Roland de Vaux, and the Jordan Department of Antiquities, then under Lankester Harding, was able to clear the site of Qumran, the monastery itself and the cave (1949 and later). A few fragments of the scrolls found and sold by the Bedouins were found in the cave.

After that there was a competition—a race, one might say—between the Bedouins, who became fully aware of the commercial value of the scrolls, and the scholars who wished to study them. We are told that in the end the

price was stabilized as one Jordanian pound (that is, one pound sterling) for every square inch of a scroll. With such an incentive, Bedouins began to search for caves. Actually, out of the eleven caves near Qumran, six were discovered by the archaeologists; but unfortunately they contained only scraps of manuscripts, and the Copper Scrolls. The Bedouins on their own discovered Caves 2, 4 and 11, all

One of the jars in which the scrolls were originally stored. (Cave 1)

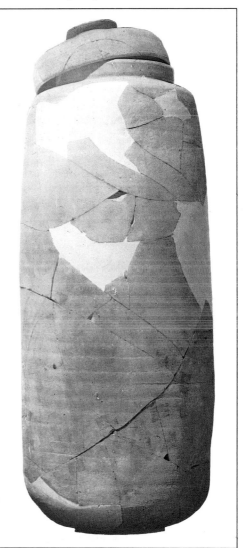

of which yielded apparently considerable results. The Bedouins from Jordan also crossed the border into Israel, and started plundering caves beyond. This illegal activity was one of the reasons for the Israel Judaean Desert Expedition of 1961. It was found that scrolls had been removed from the caves on Israeli territory; fragments later found in the plundered caves fitted closely those published by scholars abroad as of "unknown provenance." In any case this race between the Bedouins and the archaeologists may on the whole be said to have been won by the Bedouins, who had more time, energy and local knowledge. Nevertheless it yielded important results. Later on, other kinds of writings were found in the cave of Muraba'at, south of Qumran, and in the Judaean Desert Caves already mentioned.

2. The Contents of the Scrolls

The scrolls found in the Qumran caves can be divided into two groups: scrolls with biblical texts, and other writings which were composed by members of the Dead Sea Sect established at Qumran, which had been previously quite unknown.

As regards the biblical texts, fragments of every single book of the Old Testament have been found at Qumran, with the sole exception of the Book of Esther. Very many of these books were found in several copies. Two of them, Daniel and Ecclesiasticus, have been preserved in copies written only a century after the composition of the original. A relatively large number of fragments of certain biblical books were found, in which the sect was especially interested because they could be interpreted to suit its tenets. The best examples are Isaiah and the Psalms, which were actually used in the prayers of the community. The scrolls are usually written on parchment; only a few texts, for instance one of the Books of the Kings, were on papyrus. Two kinds of ink were used, the ordinary one known from antiquity which is made from lampblack and which has been more or less well preserved, and another made with some metallic addition which has unfortunately corroded the parchment. As a result in certain texts, especially in the so-called Genesis Apocryphon, the lines of writing have been eaten away and only the blank parchment in

The Manual of Discipline,
one of the seven Dead Sea Scrolls

Part of an appendix to the Manual of Discipline, dating from about 100-75 BC. The fragments had become separated and were found by archaeologists in cave 1 in Qumran.

between has been preserved. The texts are almost all in the square Hebrew writing, resembling that used in inscriptions from the end of the Second Temple period. There are a few exceptions to this rule, for instance several copies of the Book of Leviticus were written in the old Hebrew script, which the Samaritans use to this day.

In one copy of Exodus red ink has been used to mark the lines for the writing, and the headings of the various *parashot* have also been written in red. One interesting detail is that sometimes the Sacred Name of God, YHWH (pronounced 'Adonai' in Hebrew, because no one knows how to pronounce the so-called 'unutterable name' of God) was written in the old Hebrew script within a marked square.

The discoveries of these writings, which can be more or less exactly dated between the 3rd or 2nd century BC and the 2nd century AD, have been of inestimable value for our knowledge of the development of the Hebrew script.

Of course, one of the main points of interest has been the comparison of these texts with the standard Massoretic version of the Bible. These Dead Sea versions are in a very mixed state. For instance, of the two Scrolls of Isaiah found in Cave 1, one is marked by any amount of different spellings and variant versions, although on the whole it may be said that the Massoretic version (the accepted text) is usually the better one. The second Scroll of Isaiah found in the same cave is much closer to the Massoretic version.

The finds of scrolls or fragments thereof have been made so far in about half a dozen caves. Cave 1 had two Scrolls of Isaiah (one a complete one which, by the way, puts both books now regarded as First and Second Isaiah together), then fragments of the various books of the Pentateuch and three copies of the Psalms. In caves 2, 3, 5 and 6 there were a few fragments of various later Books of the Old Testament: Job, the Song of Songs, Lamentations, and three copies of the Psalms and one of the Books of the Kings written on papyrus and differing from the accepted text.

In Cave 4 there was a very rich crop of fragments. Eighteen copies of various Books of the Twelve Prophets, fourteen copies of Deuteronomy, twelve of Isaiah and ten of the Psalms.

Of special interest was the departure from the accepted versions. Thus one of the Books of Psalms preserved in the Qumran caves contains a Psalm No. 151, which was not accepted in the Canon of the Psalter. In the same way in a manuscript of Deuteronomy, the Song of Moses, which begins with the word האזינו , is longer than the usual text. There are two Scrolls of Joshua, one of which is quite similar to the Massoretic version. Scholars have established a whole pedigree of biblical texts, showing the relation between the Babylonian recension, the Egyptian version on which the Septuagint was based and the texts used in the Holy Land, and their interrelations.

Besides the biblical canonic books, the library of the Dead Sea Sect included quite a number of fragments of the so-called apochryphal books, such as the Books of the Jubilees, of Enoch, Tobias, and the Testament of Levi, which was part of the Testament of the Twelve Patriarchs. The latter appears in a different version of the accepted text, which had been known previously only in the Greek version. With these Apocrypha one can range the Commentaries written by members of the sect (the so-called *Pesharim*) on various books of the Old Testament. Fragments have been found of such commentaries on the Psalms and on the prophets Micah and Habakkuk. One of the texts which has been published so far is the Commentary on Habakkuk; it is most interesting because it illustrates the method of the Sect in commenting on the Old Testament books, which was to quote a passage from the Bible and to add that it is to be understood as referring to a certain event, or a situation which occurred in their own time; a method

still much in favour in fundamentalist circles. Of course the historic allusion in this second part of the commentary is what interests us most, for all its anachronistic character. For instance, the reference in the Commentary on Habakkuk to the Kittim is understood as meaning the Romans. This and other interpretations have been of great importance for the dating of the Sect and for an understanding of its history and its views.

As regards the Sect's own compositions quite a number of these were recovered, including one text which, paradoxically, had been known a long time before the Qumran discoveries but had never been properly understood. In 1897, together with the other fragments of the Cairo Genizah already mentioned, a fragment was found referring to some group which had passed on to "Damascus" and which apparently was led by Zadokite priests. At that time, nobody could understand to what event the whole thing referred. Now, however, in the light of the later discoveries in the Qumran caves, it has become clear that this text was also part of the original compositions of the Dead Sea Sect.

Among the scrolls found in the Qumran Cave I was also the so-called Genesis Apocryphon, published by N. Avigad and Y. Yadin; it is a commentary on the Book of Genesis of the Midrashic legendary type.

Among the writings of the Sect is the Book of the *Serakhim; Serakh* in the vocabulary of the Sect meant the rules and regulations which governed its life. This Book of *Serakhim,* or Regulations, is composed of three parts. One is the *Serakh haYahad* or Manual of Discipline, order or constitution of the community. The second is the *Serakh lekol Adath Israel Be'atid,* which means the regulations, the "Order for the whole Community of Israel at the End of the Days", the ideal constitution for the Messianic era. The third part of the *Serakhim* is the *Serakh Berakhoth,* containing the various Blessings to be said on occasions of importance to the Community.

The "Thanksgiving" Scroll before unrolling

Next in importance among the scrolls found in Cave I is a description of the "War of the Sons of Light and the Sons of Darkness" *(Megillat Milhamot Benei Or ve-Benei Hoshekh)*. This text is clearly based on the military experience of the period, but opinions are divided over whether it refers to the Hellenistic and Maccabean warfare or to the Roman times. In any case, what it describes is an apocalyptic war between those who are in the right (the Sons of Light, i.e. the Sect) and those in the wrong (the Sons of Darkness). It ends, of course, with the victory of the Sons of Light.

A third scroll also from Qumran Cave I is the so-called Thanksgiving Scroll. It contains a series of poems *(hodayoth)* written by members of the Sect which expressed their gratitude to God. Its contents are of great importance for a proper understanding of their point of view.

A word might be said about the later fate of these scrolls. As mentioned before, three of them (The "War", Isaiah 2 and the Thanksgiving Scrolls) were purchased by Sukenik, and came into the possession of the Hebrew University; they were transferred to a special building, the Shrine of the Book, which forms part of the Israel Museum. The other four (Isaiah 1, the Habakkuk Commentary, the "Manual of Discipline" and the Genesis Apocryphon) which had been bought by Mar Samuel, were taken by him to the United States; they were purchased by the Government of Israel, and finally joined the others in the Shrine of the Book.

Another scroll, so far unpublished is the so-called Temple Scroll. Its existence was brought to light after the 1967 Six-Day War. It apparently contains a description of the Temple and the City of Jerusalem as they should be in the eyes of the Sect. To complete the inventory of the scrolls, we should also mention the Copper Scrolls. These were found in Qumran Cave 4, and contain a list of huge treasures deposited in various parts of the Holy Land, but especially in Jerusalem. The text was apparently written on copper to ensure its preservation, but no one knows whether the treasures listed in it were real or imaginary. All attempts to find them have failed so far.

The "Thanksgiving" Scroll after unrolling

3. The Dead Sea Sect

We might now consider briefly the Sect itself. The Dead Sea Sect apparently rose in Maccabean times. Its founder, of whom we know only that he was called the "Teacher of Righteousness" or the "Master of Justice", was executed by a wicked High Priest—we do not know exactly to whom this refers. The Sect took refuge in "Damascus". Again, we do not know whether this refers to the actual city of that name, or to some other place figuratively called Damascus. In any case from about the time of John Hyrcanus, that is from the end of the 2nd century BC, this Sect settled at Qumran. There it built the monastery which has been excavated. It contained a quite large complex of rooms, with a great many pools for ablutions, the whole being supplied with water from the Judaean mountains. The Sect was very strongly insistent on ritual purity and hence on ritual baths. The Qumran "monastery" contained a joint *refectorium* (a place for taking meals together), a *scriptorium* (a place where people copied the scrolls), of which so many fragments have been found; these are probably only a small part of what was once really there. Qumran continued to serve as the headquarters of the Sect, with the exception of the time of King Herod. It is possible that Herod, out of opposition to the Hasmonaeans (with whom, as we shall see, the Sect was on bad terms), allowed them to live in Jerusalem. But they returned to Qumran in the time of Herod's son Archelaus, and stayed there until 68, the year in which Qumran, Jericho and its vicinity were taken by the Roman army. The monastery was then destroyed. There is some evidence of a re-settlement in the time of Bar Kochba, and after that came oblivion till 1947.

We must now add a few words concerning the Sect, as revealed in its writings. But firstly it should be clearly understood that the group was apparently a quite insignificant one; although it must have contained in the whole

Fragment of a Pentateuch Scroll from Qumran written in Palaeo-Hebrew script

course of its history several thousand members, this was not much in a Jewish population of millions. The Sect as such has left no trace in history unless we identify it with the Essenes mentioned both by Josephus and Pliny. In any case, it was a small dissident minority group which, in order to keep itself pure from worldly temptation and not to have to acknowledge what was (in its eyes) the usurpation of the Davidic Kingdom and the Zadokite High Priesthood by the Hasmonaeans, retired into the desert, the eternal refuge of outlaws and those opposed to society. It settled on the desert fringe, in the Qumran Monastery, which is possibly referred to as the Mezad Hassidim, the "Fortress of the Pious".

The basic belief of the Sect was that God had determined the fate of the world and of every human being in it from the beginning, and that His decree was irrevocable. Anyone who was numbered amongst the elect would be saved and all the others would be condemned eternally. (Naturally the members of the Sect were amongst the elect.) It did not matter how many they were; even if few, they were the people who would enjoy God's grace in a better world. In short, the Sect was based on a rigid belief in predestination, thus anticipating the teaching of Calvin by many centuries.

Secondly, the Sect held dualistic views, that is to say they believed the world to be the scene of a continuing battle between God and Satan (or, as they called him, Belial) and between the adherents of the two powers. Here again, they were of course on the side of God. As regards the actual conditions of Israel in their own times, they adhered to the Zadokite Priesthood, the ancient Aaronite family which had been deposed by the Seleucid kings. The last High Priest of this dynasty, Onias IV, had fled to Egypt. The Dead Sea Sect refused to acknowledge the legality of the Hasmonaean High Priesthood and, *a fortiori*, the legitimacy of all the High Priests appointed by Herod and his successors.

The actual High Priest was thus, in their eyes, no High Priest, and the Temple in Jerusalem was not their Temple. The true Temple would come into being at some time at the end of the world. What was still more serious for everyday life was that the Sect had its own calendar, based on a different computation from that of the other Jews. It was based on the priestly services, the "Courses" of priests which followed each other at the Temple of Jerusalem. The calendar of the Sect was not the mixed sun and moon one, as the Jewish

one was then and is at present, but was strictly a solar calendar. As a result of that divergence, the holidays of the Sect did not fall on the same days as those of the rest of the Jewish community. This of course dug a deep chasm between them and the rest of the people, because on the days that they regarded as holy all the rest of the people worked, whereas the days which the other people held as their holidays were regarded by the Qumran Sect as ordinary working days. They therefore had to live by their own rules, apart in the desert, far from the rest of the Jewish people.

The whole Dead Sea Sect was based on two groups, like two concentric circles: the Inner Group of adult males, who were full members and who were the leaders of the Sect, and an outer periphery, which included women and children, for whom the regulations were less strict. The whole Community, and especially its inner group, was organized in the most hierarchical manner. First came the Priests, then the Levites, and then the various members who were classified by merit and piety. Only full members had the right to take part in the assemblies, and share the common meals, sitting by order of merit: this was determined by the leaders of the Community and was reviewed every year. Such an annual grading of course gave the leadership of the Community an important hold on its members. Secondly, all the members of the Sect had to observe the ideology of the group in a most monolithic manner; they were not allowed any deviation, under pain of expulsion, which the Sect regarded as the equivalent of spiritual death. No one was easily admitted into the Community. There was a novitiate of two years, during which every candidate passed through two or more stages. The Inner Group practised community of goods. Every member had to hand over his worldly possessions to the Community; a special official, a sort of Inspector or Controller, was in charge of the Community property, administering it for the good of all. The Outer Group, which contained the wives and children of the members, was less strictly organized. Details of this organization have been preserved in the "Manual of Discipline" and in the Damascus document already mentioned. Among the Outer Group there was no complete community of goods in the same way as we have seen in the Inner Group. Every member had to pay the equivalent of two days' wages every month, to be distributed amongst the needy. The cemetery of Qumran, which contains bones of hundreds of women and children, served the Outer Group, at least in part.

4. The Dead Sea Sect, the Essenes and the Early Christians

The discovery of the Sect has led to a great deal of speculation, which is concentrated on two main points. One is whether the Community corresponds to the Essenes as described by Flavius Josephus in his book on the Jewish War. Josephus speaks there of the division of the Jewish people into three groups, each of which equates with a Greek philosophical school. These were the Pharisees, the Sadducees, and the Essenes. The Inner Group of the Qumran Sect certainly most resembles the Essenes as known from texts, in their insistence on celibacy, community groups and personal ritual purity. The evidence of Josephus is the more valuable, because he adds a note about the existence of an Inner Group of Essenes, differing from the rest in its views on marriage. They allowed the members to have wives and to beget children. The general consensus of scholars is that the Qumran group is identical to the Essenes. It would be very difficult to assume that there existed at the same time and at roughly the same place (for both Josephus and Pliny refer to the Desert of Judaea as the place where the Essenes lived) two or three groups with very similar views, in close proximity.

One other question which is of the highest interest is the relation between the teachings of the Dead Sea Sect (assuming them to be the

Detail of Hebrew land lease on behalf of Bar Kochba, Prince of Israel, found in the Cave of the Letters.

Essenes) and those of the early Christians. This problem has exercised the ingenuity of many scholars since 1947. There have been some who have tried to identify the Dead Sea Sect with the early Christians, but this of course is both historically and doctrinally improbable. Others have found a certain relation between the doctrines of the early Christians and those of the Dead Sea Sect. This is certainly the case in such liturgical and organizational matters as the community of goods and the meals taken in common. Various expressions found in the Thanksgiving Hymns can even be paralleled in the Sermon on the Mount, and other formulations of early Christian doctrines. We can, therefore, certainly assume that there had been contact between the two groups, and that both had a common background. Christianity, the Essenes and many other contemporary movements recorded in history were part of the general Messianic-religious ferment which characterizes the end of the Second Temple period. It was probably the result of the trauma which attended the fall of the Hasmonaean State and the subjection of the Jewish nation to Roman rule. Feeling themselves guiltless of the sin of idolatry, and yet subject to strangers, many people at that time despaired of society and soon turned to a hope of Messianic salvation.

Jesus, of course, might have known of the Qumran Sect, if we accept the localization of the Baptism in the Jordan near Jericho and that of the Wilderness (to which Jesus retreated for forty days) in the mountain nearby. Certainly John the Baptist may well have preached and baptized people in the Jordan not very far from the site of the Qumran Monastery; the Christians would thus have had ample opportunity to get to know the Sect and its tenets. But it is equally certain that the two movements gradually grew apart, the Dead Sea Sect sinking into oblivion and Christianity starting on its historical career.

The relation of the Essenes with the Jewish community of their time is another matter. On this point there is much contradiction of what we know of the Essenes and what Josephus Flavius tells us. Following his favourite pattern of paralleling the various Jewish ideologies with the current Greek philosophies, the Essenes correspond in Josephus' scheme to the cynics because of their detachment from society and their abhorrence of the organized state. One would, therefore, expect them to follow a pacifist policy in the conflict with the Romans. Actually the evidence found at Masada, where fragments of several writings of the Qumran Community were found, suggests the contrary—a collaboration of the Essenes with the Zealots. Josephus himself mentions that a certain Essene was commander of one of the military districts set up in the time of the First Revolt against Rome. The Essenes seem, therefore, to have taken in 66 A.D. a position in favour of the war with the Romans. Certainly the Scroll of the War of the Sons of Light with the Sons of Darkness does not indicate any pronounced pacifist leanings. It is quite possible, therefore, that the members of the Qumran Sect took part in the general uprising against the Romans in 66.

Another problem that has been raised recently is that of their real relation to some of the members of the Hasmonaean dynasty. It has been generally assumed that the "Wicked Priest" who executed the Master of Justice was King Alexander Jannaeus, whom Josephus reports to have crucified thousands of his opponents. However, a new text, part of the Temple Scroll already mentioned, was published and interpreted by Y. Yadin. It suggests that the Essenes were entirely opposed to the views of the Pharisees, the main opponents of King Alexander; in fact they dubbed them "those who speak smoothly", accusing them of hypocrisy.

From the same text it appears that the members of the Dead Sea Sect agreed with the Sadducee interpretation of the Torah, at least as far as the execution of criminals is concerned. The accepted version in the bibli-

The waterskin in which the Bar Kochba letters were found.

cal text was that when a man was condemned to death he should first be executed and then his body should be exposed on a "tree" (a wooden pole). The Sadducees interpreted this verse differently; they followed another version, according to which the criminal was to be set up on a pole (that is "crucified") while still alive, and this evidently was the opinion of the Sect itself. Possibly, also, the "Young Lion" or the "Lion's whelp" who is mentioned in the commentary on Habakkuk is a complimentary reference to Alexander Jannaeus and not the contrary, as has been believed hitherto. This interpretation would agree well with the known fact of the participation of the Essenes in the Zealots' War against the Romans.

In a certain sense, of course, the discovery of the scrolls in the Qumran caves has distorted our historical perspective about the later period of the Second Temple, more or less in the same manner in which the history of the Near East in the Hellenistic and Early Roman periods has been distorted by the mass of original sources in the Egyptian papyri. As we know so much more about matters which are recorded in the available sources, our attention is focused on them and we are inclined to magnify their historical effect. The pitiful fragments of the library of Qumran allow us to imagine the quantity of writings

which existed at that time in Judaea, of which only feeble remnants have come down to our time in the shape of the various Apocrypha. Taken judiciously, the finds of the Qumran scrolls are historically interesting; but we should not exaggerate the importance of the Essenes in Jewish history as distinct from that of the Christian church. The Essenes lived apart from the main stream of Jewish life. They did not and could not influence historical events in a decisive manner, however interesting their works may be intrinsically.

5. Other Discoveries in the Judaean Desert Caves

The discovery of the Qumran manuscripts has, of course, done much to stimulate research in the other caves of the Judaean Desert. We have already mentioned the "research" made by the Bedouins on both sides of the Armistice lines which existed between Israel and Jordan from 1948 to 1967. These depredations motivated an Israeli expedition to the caves in the vicinity of En-Gedi. Its work went on in the winters of 1960 and 1961. There were four groups of researchers, each led by a well-known archaeologist. From our point of view the most successful one was the group led by Professor Yadin, who worked in

Cave D, on the south side of the Hever valley. The cave, in the course of time, received the name of the "Cave of the Letters", and for good reason. It served as a refuge for a group of rebels from the time of Bar Kochba, the Jewish leader in the Second Roman War. Among those hiding in the cave was at least one of the administrators of the Community of En-Gedi, who were in charge of the region on behalf of Bar Kochba. After the defeat they fled to these inaccessible caves and stayed there for some time. The Romans were unable to attack them directly; hence they set up camps on top of the cliffs above the caves, hoping in this way to starve the refugees out. The fate of the different groups who had fled the caves varied. In one case a cave near En-Gedi itself seems to have been provided with a water supply and it is quite possible that the people who hid in it did escape in the end. In another cave, aptly named the "Cave of Horrors", the refugees refused to surrender. When they had no more means of subsistence they collected all their goods into one vast pyre so as to leave nothing to the conquerors and then committed mass suicide. The fate of the group which had fled to the "Cave of the Letters" is unknown. The fact that no coins or jewels were found in the cave (although a jewel box was there) might indicate either that they surrendered or that they succeeded in escaping. In any case they left their archives in the cave to be found centuries later.

The archives found in the cave were of two kinds. Firstly, Jonathan, one of the rebel commanders of En-Gedi, took with him the letters which he had received from Bar Kochba's headquarters. These documents are an invaluable commentary on the way of administration of the revolutionary government. They show that the Bar Kochba administration was conducted in a most orderly manner, probably with the help of scribes trained in the Hellenistic official procedure. There seems to have been a central registry in every district. Documents were issued by it

dated to the year so-and-so, of the Era of Freedom and for Redemption of Israel by Simeon, the son of Kossibah, the Prince (Nassi) of Israel. Ben Kossibah is apparently the real name of Bar Kochba, which had not been known before. The various leases issued in Bar Kochba's name show that the Roman imperial estates were taken over by the new government and leased out to various groups of people or individuals in an orderly administrative way. This actually went on for the whole three years of the revolt; the last documents are dated to the year four—although this is probably a misconstruction of the scribe who believed the era of Bar Kochba to begin in the spring (Nissan), and not in the autumn (Tishri), as was actually the case. We obtain from these texts many glimpses of the way in which Bar Kochba conducted his government. We have the usual letters of recommendations of certain people to the local rulers. One man, a certain Eliashar, is sent to En-Gedi. The local governor, Jonathan, is told to do whatever Eliashar tells him; he should help Eliashar as far as possible.

In another document the local commander asks for a person, one Eleazer Bar Hitta, to be brought before him immediately even before the Sabbath. In a third document Bar Kochba reproaches the En-Gedi commander: "You sit, eat and drink from the property of the house of Israel and care nothing for your brethren"; the same letter refers also to a ship, which shows that En-Gedi was one of the centres of supply of the rebels.

We learn quite a lot about the religious zeal of the men of Bar Kochba. For instance, special men were sent to En Gedi to collect palm branches and citrons (etrogim) for the Festival of the Tabernacles; others were to bring myrtles and willows, all of which were to be tithed, and then sent to the camp. Apparently the matter of having the right lulav for the feast of Tabernacles aroused the interest of the highest authorities. In spite, however, of this religious tenor of the revolt, the army of

Bar-Kochba was not composed exclusively of Jews. (We know of this also from other literary sources.) There was apparently in the army of Bar-Kochba quite a number of non-Jews or Hellenized Jews, who had to be addressed in Greek and to whom headquarters gave orders in Greek. For instance, one Ananuns or Hananiya writes in Greek to Jonathan, greeting him as his "brother." The soldiers of Bar-Kochba were apparently formed into "Bands of Brothers," who faced the enemy together. In other documents, we see how the local commanders are ordered to bring before Bar-

Kochba a certain Thyrsis, the son of Kilianus, a purely Roman name, for "We need him."

This group of documents found at the Cave of Letters in Hever valley fits in well with another group of documents from the time of Bar-Kochba or somewhat earlier which were found in the Cave of Mubara'at, between Qumran and En Gedi. These are composed mostly of legal documents, leases and marriage contracts, all of which throw very interesting light on the conditions of life in the time of Bar-Kochba. Thus for instance we have a document stating that on the 20th Shvat, Year

One of the Bar Kochba's letters found at Wadi Mubara'at

2 of the Liberation of Israel by authority of Simeon son of Kossibah, the Prince of Israel, in the District of Herodium (that is the old Herodium Fortress) certain acts were carried out by a representative of Bar Kochba. These include a contract of sublease between a certain Elazar the son of Shiloni and Hillel the son of Garas concerning a property at some place called Nahash. Here too was found a document in which the local commander in the Jericho region is asked to bring certain men urgently to Bar Kochba. Bar Kochba calls upon Joshua the son of Galgula and the people of Habaruch invoking Heaven as a witness, that if anything should befall the Galileans who are with them, he would put them in irons as he did to one Aphlas. In another letter people are sent from headquarters to collect five bushels of wheat. They are to be well received, should stay with Joshua for the Sabbath and all should be done to make them satisfied. The wheat is to be delivered the day after the Sabbath. The local commander is to be told at the same time "to be strong and strengthen the hearts of those placed in your charge." There was even found in Mubara'at one letter from Jonathan in En-Gedi (well known to us from the Hever finds) to a certain Joseph, recommending to him one Euphrosius, the son of Elazar, a very charitable man, who has given to the poor, and who requires a gift of... (there is a blank here).

We now return to the second set of archives found in the Cave of Letters. These are document which once belonged to a woman called Babata, the daughter of Simeon and Miriam. She lived at Zoar at the south end of the Dead Sea and found refuge at En-Gedi. As she was a relative of Jonathan, the commander there, she later on fled with him to a cave. From the private archives of Babata, which contain texts in Hebrew, Nabatean and Greek, we can reconstruct the whole life history of this woman. Her father endowed her mother, Miriam, with all his possessions; these passed on to Babata. She had to declare them under oath to the Land Census of the Province of Arabia, because her property was situated in the district of Rabbat Moab. Babata was married twice. By her first husband, one Joshua the son of Joseph, she had a child: Joshua the son of Joshua, who is the subject of many legal documents, concerning her property and the right of guardianship over him. After the death of her first husband Babata married a certain Jehuda son of Eleazer, who came from En-Gedi. He died almost immediately after the marriage, leaving Babata a large property. The latter was claimed by his relatives as belonging to the founder of the family, Eleazar son of Judah, and not to his son Jehuda. Before marrying Babata, her second husband had been the husband of another woman from En-Gedi, one Miriam the daughter of Bayan; as the local commander at En Gedi was Joshua the son of Bayan, a link was thus created which endured throughout the war. By his first wife Judah had a daughter called Shlomzion and she too had property claims. As a result of these complications a whole correspondence passed between the various families and the many documents connected with Babata's life can be brought into focus.

The finds in the Hever valley are not the last finds of papyri made, even if we disregard the Temple Scroll as it belongs to the Qumran finds. There has been a find of important papyri in a cave in the Wadi Daliya, north-west of Jericho. It contained one of the earliest collections of documents so far discovered in Palestine. Apparently the cave in the Wadi Daliya served as refuge to Samaritans who at the beginning of the Hellenistic period had fled from their city of Samaria into the desert, pursued by Macedonian soldiers.We know from other sources that the Samaritans had revolted against Alexander the Great and that either he or the Regent Perdiccas, who governed after the king's death, had settled a colony of Macedonian veterans in Samaria. Apparently the original inhabitants of Samaria, including the family of Sanbalay, hereditary governor of the city, fled from it, taking with them various documents, some dating to the Persian and others to the early Hellenistic period. The refugees were surrounded in the cave, and quite possibly killed by smoke. In any case, two hundred skulls were found in the cave, together with many documents. Most of these finds are still unpublished.

Scholars have been working on the scrolls of the Holy Land from all directions. Philologists have studied the language of these documents, and reconstructed the kinds of dialects spoken in Judaea and Galilee at that time, in particular that known as Western Aramaic. The legal implications of these documents are also very important, and have to be studied in the light of Roman Law and of the Jewish Law of the Mishna and the Talmud. Then there is the problem of the Nabataean administrative practices. Some of the documents of Babata are still dated by the reign of Rabel II, the last King of the Nabataeans. Petra was apparently the seat of the court which dealt with her property situated in the District of Zoar. Hence her archives contained Nabataean documents, side by side with Greek documents, issued after the Romans had taken over the province in 106 AD.

There is also the question of the various aspects of the religious and social developments. From the period of the Greek conquest by Alexander come the Wadi Daliya documents, according to which slaves are bought and sold, to the latest documents from the Bar Kochba period and even beyond them the Byzantine documents of Nessana.

Conclusions

Before we can judge the importance of these finds, we should remember that a lot of these documents are as yet unpublished, and even after publication the correct text must first be established and the various possible readings considered. Then and only then can these documents be properly evaluated. Finally, we must always remember that they allow us only a very narrow, although authentic, glimpse of what happened in the past. Like all chance-finds of this sort they give us only the details, the trees and not the forest. All this mass of material has not only to be properly digested but also to be evaluated, because although undoubtedly authentic, these documents show us perhaps only one-thousandth, perhaps even less, of what really went on.

Actually it is only the historian, able to lift himself above this mass of small details and possessing a wide general knowledge and understanding of the period, who can fit in this new knowledge and derive full profit from this new material.

We see that almost everything we know about antiquity is derived either from manuscripts transmitted through the ages, or other writings (inscriptions, papyri or parchments) found in the course of excavations. The art of the future historian must be to combine the knowledge derived from these two sources, in order to obtain a just and balanced view of what really happened in the past, where lie the origins of so many determinant factors of present-day thought.

Index

Bibliography

1. Cole, Dan P. Dead Sea Scrolls. Shanks, Hershel, ed. 1993, Biblical Archaeological Society.

2. Cook, Edward M. Solving the Mysteries of the Dead Sea Scrolls: New Light on the Bible. 1994, Zondervan Publishing Co.

3. Eisenman, Robert and Wise, Michael. The Dead Sea Scrolls Uncovered. 1993, Viking Penguin

4. Golb, Norman. Who Wrote the Dead Sea Scrolls? The Search for the Meaning of the Qumran Manuscripts (illus.). 1995, Macmillan Publ. Co.

5. Scrolls: Forty Years of Research. (Studies on the Texts of the Desert of Judah: Vol. 10) 1992, Brill, E.J.

6. Shanks, Hershel, ed. Understanding the Dead Sea Scrolls: A Reader. 1993, Random House Inc.

7. Sussman, Ayalah & Peled, Ruth. Scrolls from the Dead Sea. 1993, Braziller, George, Inc.

8. Vanderkam, James. The Dead Sea Scrolls Today (illus.). 1994, Eerdmans, William B., Publishing Co.

9. Vermes, Geza. The Dead Sea Scrolls in English. 1988, Viking Penguin.

lO. Yadin' Yigael. The Message of the Scrolls. 1991, Crossroad Publishing Co.